Babies as People
NEW FINDINGS
ON OUR SOCIAL BEGINNINGS

Due

Babies as People

NEW FINDINGS
ON OUR SOCIAL BEGINNINGS

Edward Tronick
& Lauren Adamson

COLLIER BOOKS
A Division of Macmillan Publishing Co., Inc.
NEW YORK

Collier Macmillan Publishers
LONDON

created by Media Projects Incorporated

Macmillan Publishing Co., Inc.
866 Third Avenue, New York, N.Y. 10022
Collier Macmillan Canada, Ltd.

Library of Congress Cataloging in Publication Data

Tronick, Edward.
  Babies as people.

    1. Infant psychology. 2. Infants (Newborn)
I. Adamson, Lauren, joint author.   II. Title.
BF719.T76 1980   155.4′22   80-14355
ISBN: 0-02-078070-2

Designed by Mary Gale Moyes

First Collier Books Edition 1980

Printed in United States of America

Contents

Acknowledgments

A book, like a baby, develops in a social context. Both must eventually stand alone, but to do so, they initially depend on others for support and guidance. During this project, many people offered us such aid. We are especially indebted to T. Berry Brazelton, whose unmatched ability to peer into the infant's world was a powerful inspiration to us. We are also grateful to Heidelise Als, and the other colleagues with whom we worked at the Child Development Unit, for the creative and critical stimulation they provided us during our years there.

Sara B. Stein was instrumental in the writing of this book from its very inception, and without her it might not have been. With her acute editorial judgment, her ready wit, and her unfailing insight, she guided and goaded us.

We owe considerable debts to our families, though these are more difficult to reckon. Just by sharing their lives with us, Anna and Daniel have continually forced us to question all easy explanations about them. Denise and Wally gave us their thoughts, and never failed to provide us space and comfort as we worked.

And lastly, we must acknowledge the parents and infants who participated in our studies and in the studies of others. They have willingly shared in our endeavors. We hope most of all that they find value in this book.

Introduction

I wish I'd written this book. It was delightful to read, and I found myself identifying with both reader and authors. It should be an eminently rewarding book for all new parents, for it attempts, in a style that is warm and understanding, to make the rapidly increasing volume of infant research intelligible and useful.

I have worked closely with both authors and value their research abilities. I know they understand infants and I believe their having recently had children of their own is a valuable asset to them as interpreters of the new research. They are able to present these findings in a way that makes them equally valid for parents, psychologists, pediatricians, nurses, teachers—whoever might want to play with new babies. Having two authors of different sexes also adds a subtle but important dimension: The interests of each parent are brought to play on this complex and fascinating creature —the baby human.

My own research interests have centered on the individuality of each baby and on how that might influence parents.

I'd hoped that establishing an understanding of how individuality comes about might then provide us, as clinicians interested in improving the quality of life for babies and their parents, with the necessary insights to help parents "make it" better with their babies. If parents make it with their babies, they also begin to feel better about themselves. And, if they feel good about parenting, this is passed on to the baby. The baby begins to feel rewarded as a person. In other words, parents' self-images directly affect their infants'. When parents are at ease with themselves, their joy in the baby is multiplied. Since, in our nuclear families, there are fewer individualized backups for parents these days, and more occasions for confusion about child-rearing practices, I have been looking for ways to encourage them in their capacities as parents.

One of the surest backups, one which is constantly present and is individualized for each parent, is the baby. If parents can be freed of the inhibitions placed on them by our competitive society and by their wish to do the "perfect" job by their baby, they can begin to look at the baby—to value the baby's responses and to see in them the key to their constant question, "Am I doing right by my child?" But this is not easy, for we have been taught over generations that a baby is essentially incompetent and that we are solely and irrevocably responsible for the infant's future. Neither of these assumptions is, however, true. We have merely been blinded from seeing the nonverbal language of infant responses; but present research begins to teach us how to "read" a small baby. This book, a pleasure and a reassuring reference for new parents, will further help parents reach that goal.

As soon as the baby—even the fetus and the newborn—can be accepted as an active participant in parent-infant interaction, the responsive language becomes impressively enriched. The feedback that parents receive when correctly reading their baby lets them know how important they are to their child. Infants clearly differentiate very early between mothers and fathers. They respond in predictable, special ways to each parent, locking each parent to them. This implies, of course, that each parent is watching and is ready to be locked in. We can videotape a playful interaction between a four-week-old baby and both parents. So pervasive is this specialized behavioral system of interaction that, by observing the movement of the baby's toe or finger over a two-minute sequence, we can predict with a very high degree of accuracy which parent is in the baby's play space. The baby's whole body behaves differently for each parent. And, once a parent is aware of these differences, it is difficult not to become "hooked."

The processes which fuel a small baby's development have interested me for a long time. The growth and maturation of the central nervous system is the captain of this progress. We can see this from what happens when the nervous system's ability to receive and utilize information and to discharge it by appropriate motor response is not intact. In such cases the development of the child is bound to be impaired or disorganized, and the problems for the child and for the parents are multiplied. We are finding that brain-damaged children can make remarkable recoveries with appropriate stimulation; but development is likely to be slow and more tortuous.

The second force for development comes from the baby's own genetic makeup. The human baby is programmed genetically to safeguard his or her survival by responding to sensory and social stimuli and mastering motor skills, such as locomotion. A baby works systematically to achieve each developmental step. When a baby completes a task, one can see an "Ha!" phenomenon—"At last! I've done it!" Feedback from success fuels the next step. Robert White has called this an inner "sense of competence" that is further nourished with each new achievement.

The third force in development is that provided by parents and other nurtural people in the baby's environment. As the baby works to achieve social competence or to act on the environment, the reinforcement that a parent or an older child offers critically affects the degree of satisfaction the baby gets from each progressive step. If the nurturing people are observant and supportive, the infant's excitement and ability to concentrate and persevere are naturally heightened.

Rewarding feedback is powerfully reinforcing. Without this, development comes to a halt in early infancy. An institutionalized baby of four to five months may begin to lose necessary motivation for motor and social progress, turning inward in what Rene Spitz has called an anaclytic depression. The baby may cease to make efforts toward developmental progress, and appear to be depressed and distracted. This can be so pervasive that the body may slow its growth and become unable to handle even minor infections. Many such babies die from being overwhelmed by minor respiratory infections. All of the baby's systems are directly fueled by and dependent upon nurturance from without as well as from within.

This book will fuel parents, giving them insights into their baby's internal mechanisms. This understanding can help them provide the best possible environment for their very "special" baby. Fortunately, this is in no way a "how-to" book—it has always seemed to me that the assumption behind such books is that the authority knows it all, and the parents don't. I have worked with parents for too many years to believe that. My respect is enormous for their capacity to read the individuality of their own infant, and to couple that insight with their own goals for that baby. This book will act to further such understanding and deepen the personal rewards of dedicated parents.

T. Berry Brazelton
Children's Hospital Medical Center
Harvard Medical School
Boston, Massachusetts

The author of this introduction is supported by the Robert Wood Johnson Foundation, the Carnegie Corporation, and the National Institute of Mental Health.

Babies as People
NEW FINDINGS
ON OUR SOCIAL BEGINNINGS

1. Introducing the Baby Human

In our society, adults have few opportunities to test their care-giving skills before they must take responsibility for their first baby. Before they become parents, they may wonder how they will ever learn to nurture such an immature and dependent human being. Will they know what he needs and wants? How can they introduce him to all the complexities of human existence? If they make "mistakes," can they be corrected? And, despite the advice of countless how-to parent manuals and the counsel of experienced friends, they may fear they will never come up with satisfactory answers in time.

But once the child is born, parents soon discover they have a most unexpected teacher—their new baby. They marvel at how different he or she is from the image they spent nine months pondering. It is not that their baby is miraculously independent or mature. Nor is it that the baby is non-demanding; they may, in fact, think their newborn asks far more than they dreamed possible. Yet this very demanding-ness seems to be the key: it guides their every care-giving effort.

Parenthood involves a partnership with a baby, an intimate sharing and mutual shaping of each moment. Here, for example, is a description of Lynn and her newborn son Matthew, greeting each other during one of their midnight encounters.

> Matthew stirs. His arms stretch upward and then, as he arches his back, they fling jerkily outward. When his tiny fists thump the crib bars, he whimpers softly. Lynn wakens immediately and promptly rises. As her milk begins to flow, she realizes that despite her fatigue and soreness, she is eager to hold her baby. As Lynn approaches the crib, Matthew's whimper is escalating into a vigorous cry, and his face contorts into a tense grimace. She leans over him and whispers, "I'm here, Matty, don't cry." He relaxes immediately. His limb movements become smooth and controlled. Tension drains from his face and he opens one eye and then the next. Mother and baby gaze wide-eyed at each other. Lynn beams a special, comically exaggerated smile; Matthew smiles, sighs, then turns away to mouth his now-still fist. She strokes his cheek and utters a short, high-pitched singsong. He glances back at her briefly and fusses softly. Gently she picks him up. He eagerly molds his small body to hers. . . .

Throughout this brief scene Lynn acts as if Matthew is able to engage in social interchange. She doesn't seem to regard their conversation as a sham in which she is performing for a passive audience. If we were to challenge Lynn's assumptions, she could point to convincing evidence Matthew provides.

One of Lynn's assumptions is that Matthew lives in our world of sights, sounds, and touches—and she doesn't hesitate to provide him with a personal display of the wealth of those sensations. He in turn seems to demonstrate that she is right, for he stills to her voice, gazes up at her face, and molds his body to hers when she picks him up.

Moreover, Lynn does not treat Matthew as a passive consumer of all this outside stimulation. She watches him to see how he digests it and how, in his own baby way, he comments on it. She tries to read his replies and respond appropriately. For instance, Matthew smiled briefly during their initial greeting, then turned away to suck his fist. When Lynn recalled his gaze by stroking and singsonging—but didn't immediately replace his fist with a more satisfying object—Matthew fussed as if to say, "Yes, hi, Mom, but now feed me." Lynn got the message and promptly cut short her prelude.

Parents are often amazed that their new baby is such a good partner that, from the very beginning, he uses his array of infant ways to tell them what he wants and how they might best provide it. By Matthew's first birthday, Lynn fondly remembered the ritual of "getting up in the middle of the night." Of course, the necessary night feeding reflected the devotion and selflessness care-giving entails. But it also symbolized to Lynn the perplexing relationship her baby demanded—and it provided her with a source of invaluable information. As Lynn observed Matthew's movements and moods, she learned to decode his signals long before he could use conventional gestures and words. So, although his first actions were not nearly so sophisticated as his rich one-year-old repertoire, they were nonetheless communicative. Since Lynn could understand them, they formed the basis for an intimate dialogue that gradually changed to suit her baby's growing capacities.

Lynn could also see how, despite his countless changes during that first year, Matthew remained a unique individual. She sensed from the very start that he had a coherent personality which contributed to the form and content of their special relationship. This relationship seemed to flow continuously. Only a few striking milestones, such as his first "real" smiles and his long-awaited "mama," punctuated this stream of continual transformation. Matthew was, of course, developing but he was also providing a basic theme across the transformations. Lynn came to understand these themes as she became acquainted with her baby's personal preferences.

Not long ago, such maternal wisdom found little confirmation in scholarly works about early psychological development. "Mothers," such tomes might read, "may fancy that they are really communicating with their babies. But the facts refute such tender flights of imagination." Presumably, newborn infants were unable to perceive the world well enough to make any sense of it, much less to communicate their feelings and intentions to others.

Now parents are not the only adults convinced of—and amazed by—how well babies communicate. This idea has recently gained wide acceptance among professionals who study the beginnings of psychological development. Many avenues of research have been converging over the past decade to press upon us a view of human newborns as delightfully tuned-in social creatures, outfitted with winning ways intended to ensure the social and physical nurturing they require. Their actions speak to all who listen. While caregivers comprehend their babies' unusual vocabulary and help them fulfill their first developmental goals, researchers can analyze infant behavior in order to achieve a fuller understanding of what a baby's world is like.

Can adults ever know what a newborn baby experiences? We surely can create amusing and surprising pictures of a baby's world simply by pretending we are infant-sized. Try to pretend, for example, that you are Matthew during the scene previously described.

A gnawing sensation arouses you from a deep sleep. Still not fully awake, your body is enveloped in anguish. Its source is difficult to determine—is it your stomach, your bowels? You emit a piercing, rhythmic cry. All your movements reinforce your aimless efforts to rid yourself of your discomfort. Suddenly a singing, smiling giant appears and embraces you while proffering warm milk.

Even when we transform our perspective so markedly, we conjure up only a first approximation of Matthew's impression of this event. To fully enter his world, we would have to alter our minds as well as our physical size. We'd have to abandon all words and forget all memories: we would have no help identifiying either the giant or the milk. It may be that even our most basic assumptions about objects and space, time and causality would have to be relinquished. Perhaps the giant wouldn't even seem to be a whole person. Maybe we wouldn't realize that she was not part of our own body. Could it be that all we would experience during this whole episode would be a multitude of disconnected sensations, a jumble of soft touches, hazy blurs, and aching organs?

Generations of adults have delighted in such thought experiments. Those who perform them professionally have drawn some intriguing sketches of our first glimpses of reality. But their pictures rarely depict the same scene. One image which has been popular is that of philosopher and psychologist William James. He proposed that the infant experiences a bizarre world, for, "assailed by eyes, ears, nose, skin and entrails at once, [he] feels that all is one great booming, buzzing confusion." Others suggest a very different early existence. For example, many medical authorities have implied that the baby inhabits an isolated niche devoid of most sounds and of all the sights we adults take for granted. While James thought of babies as cognitively confused, in this view they are mercifully sheltered. Their immature brains cannot even register all the sensory information that bombards them. Indeed, newborns, it was once suggested, might even be spared the displeasure of hearing their own screaming pleas for help by fluid that clogs their ears!

Even though these two extreme views are astonishingly different, they both rest on certain suppositions about what newborns are like. Basically, these thought experiments picture babies negatively, as passive and disorganized. In both versions, babies enter the world unprepared to meet its challenges. They lack the skills to control their emotions and their actions. Adults must therefore guide them, expecting few suggestions about what to do from the babies themselves. In turn—and in time—these helpless babies become what we make them, and/or what their own internal maturation processes dictate.

Such ideas are certainly capable of fueling the fears and doubts expressed by many prospective parents. After all, parents are the people who must shape such helpless humans. If a baby is inherently disorganized, then the structure parents provide becomes singularly significant. They not only have to foster development, they literally have to mold its course.

Babies are only rarely consulted by armchair ponderers when the latter perform their thought experiments. To perform a thought experiment—to imagine what the world must look and feel like from a baby's perspective—can lead to as many different pictures as there are adult imaginations. Given such different pictures, how are we to decide whose thought experiment leads us best into the infant's world? Which are plausible descriptions, and which fanciful pictures?

Maybe babies themselves can tell us—if, that is, we are clever enough to structure situations which let their actions speak. Many researchers are now adopting this strategy and it seems to be paying off. Babies, of course, rarely offer simple, clear answers to our questions. But with the exciting hints they do provide, we can begin to separate plausible descriptions of their experience from mere flights of our adult-sized imaginations.

An experiment we recently completed at Children's Hospital in Boston illustrates what babies can tell us if we consult them. We "asked" a number of infants if they could unscramble how an object feels from its visual properties. We found this question interesting because many psychologists have assumed that they can't, although these professionals give very different reasons for their views. For example, T.G.R. Bower, an extremely clever British researcher, argues that babies first perceive objects as globs of sensation: they get the general picture but are unaware that it is made up of different pieces, some derived from their sense of touch and others from vision. The world-famous Jean Piaget strongly disagrees. Babies, he suggests, may sense the pieces, but they cannot put them together. They only come to understand an object when they can act on it by reaching out and touching it, for instance, or by tracking its movements with their eyes. Very young infants act in such an uncoordinated way, he says, that they are not yet able to realize that the object they touch may well be the same object they are looking at.

What we did was to invite babies between the ages of two days and three months to act as judges. The courtroom was our laboratory where our judges could be comfortable and undistracted in their own special infant seats. We waited patiently until they were alert and calm. Then we watched their reactions when their eyes and foreheads were lightly covered by two different cloths. One cloth was opaque so that when the babies felt it over their faces it also blocked their vision. The other cloth was exactly the same except it was transparent. We wanted to know, you might say, if such young babies could tell the difference between a blindfold and a pair of glasses.

The more we listened to what our tiny judges told us, the more we recognized that neither Bower nor Piaget would leave our court unscathed. The babies all became agitated when the opaque cloth blocked their vision: they vigorously twisted their heads, cycled their arms and legs, arched their backs, and even cried. The transparent cloth, by contrast, seemed hardly to bother them at all. Contrary to Bower's suggestion, our babies seemed to be differentiating between two objects solely on the basis of what they saw, as distinguished from what they felt.

The evidence against Piaget is far more subtle and certainly less convincing. We had to watch the videotapes we made of the babies over and over again in slow motion. First, we found that even though very young babies certainly couldn't play a skillful game of peek-a-boo with the opaque cloth, their efforts were not entirely clumsy. They were able to locate the cloth: they brought their hands near it repeatedly and many even swiped directly at it. And the babies startled us with their quick reactions. As soon as the babies cried (often after only half a minute), we removed the opaque cloths from their faces. Since they were contorting their faces into grimaces, their eyes were closed and they could not see what had happened. Nevertheless, these babies calmed down in less than five seconds, relaxed in their easy chairs, and resumed looking around. Just by sensing a tactile change, they seemed to infer that their view had changed as well. In this case, at least, babies appeared to coordinate touch and sight much more fully than Piaget imagined.

An important part of Piaget's picture does, however, stand up well in this court: his strong insistence that a baby's own actions play a critical role in how the baby knows the world at any given moment. This idea is supported by a very curious mistake all our babies made when the transparent cloth was covering their eyes. If they happened to close their eyes, they made exactly the same kind of twists and swipes they would have performed if the opaque cloth, rather than the transparent one, had been covering their eyes. While we researchers couldn't fool the babies into scrambling up touches and sights, they could fool themselves by jumbling up the results of their own actions with the properties of an object.

So, what is the verdict? Here we have to be very careful. We are not in a real court of law; we cannot be sure we have understood our judges' final decree. One trial can never stand alone—it is merely a small part of a long sequence of appeals. But we can use these new clues as we try again to imagine the baby's first world.

Take our clue about the babies' valiant efforts to get rid of the opaque blindfolds and their apparent relief when they made us remove them for them by crying. This may indicate that in their everyday world, populated by care-giving giants, they make equally vigorous attempts to look around. And, if they cannot find a good vantage point by themselves, they may cry out their requests so that the care-giver finds a vantage point for them. Perhaps, then, babies don't live in such isolated niches after all. Maybe they want to explore the world visually, and maybe they come equipped with a noise-maker so that they can communicate this desire to helpful adults.

We have another clue that suggests all is not a "booming, buzzing confusion" either. At least in some moods, babies may be able to unjumble such senses as vision and touch to connect pieces of information they pick up in different ways about the same object. It is conceivable that at times they can enjoy their care-givers' loving embraces and exciting faces as portions of the same fantastic experience.

Now, one final clue. Young babies probably experience themselves and the world without knowing who or what is responsible for what they are sensing. They do get confused, as when we saw them transform the transparent cloth into the much less desirable opaque one simply by closing their own eyes. If babies continue to make such mistakes when we ask them to preside over future trials, we will have to paint their world using a qualitatively different style than we use for our own. In this first world, perhaps there is no boundary between the baby and the world outside himself, at least from the tiny infant's perspective.

Just as you don't parent a "thought baby" as you learn to care for an infant, so researchers are unable to understand babies by performing only thought experiments. As more and more babies are actually consulted, researchers realize that a full picture of the newborn will have to incorporate their many abilities for relating to their new world. Much work still needs to be done before a complete understanding is achieved (and perhaps we will never really be able to unravel all the mysteries), but two things are now quite apparent.

First, we have learned so much already from babies that we can no longer accept any pictures that display them as primarily passive and disorganized. Rather, they have shown us that they actively organize themselves from the moment of birth—and almost certainly before. Our basic concept of who babies are has undergone a total revision. As Robert Emde, a research psychiatrist, recently remarked, the "study babies" of today and the "thought babies" of just twenty years ago are so dissimilar we might mistake them for members of two different species.

Second, researchers are coming to regard babies in much the same light as new parents like Lynn do. Babies are competent communicators. They fit with their care-givers as partners engaged in common tasks; they organize their behavior to contribute actively to a budding relationship. The baby asks for action—not only feedings, but also smiles and cuddles, certain postures, facial expressions, and tones of voice—and the adult answers. The care-giver comes to expect comments on these answers so that he or she has some basis for planning future actions.

Of course, even if babies and adults are partners in a rich social life, they are certainly not equals. Babies are not "miniature adults" trapped inside smaller and less coordinated exteriors. Our task is therefore exceedingly difficult: we must figure out how babies are organized in a way that is vastly different from the way we are. We have to know both what they can't do that we do effortlessly, and what they do in ways we have long since forgotten. Moreover, we need to understand how two people, the baby and the adult, can meet one another and communicate successfully enough that the child's development proceeds smoothly even though the two structure their worlds in such different ways.

Much of the researcher's effort is directed to making explicit the very same mechanisms parents spend so much time fostering. What parents perceive and ponder, researchers try to describe and interpret. Parents aim for an on-going relationship with their baby, and so must remain deeply immersed in the interaction. Researchers can step outside such active involvement with a particular baby (indeed they must struggle to remain objective and to divorce their hopes and dreams from their observations—a goal most researchers find impossible with their own infants). Researchers also have a storehouse of methods with which to observe and probe infant behavior. Yet, much of the time, the events researchers probe are true-to-life episodes, scenes not much different from Lynn and Matthew's conversing at midnight.

Heidelise Als, a research psychologist and one of our colleagues at Children's Hospital in Boston, spent many months, for instance, analyzing what goes on as mothers feed their babies. Like all observers who try to study complex events, she had to deal with a number of major obstacles, not the least of which was how to handle the enormous wealth of information she could collect from even a single feeding. To keep track of everything important that went on, Als made a long list of behavior patterns a baby and a mother could possibly demonstrate in such a situation. Is the baby awake? Crying?

Looking at the mother? Is the mother singing? Cuddling? Smiling? In total, she listed over a hundred different possibilities.

Then she had to consider her time scale. If she tried to take notes every five seconds, she would go insane; every five minutes, she would lose too much information. After trying out different time intervals, Als compromised at fifteen seconds. Every fifteen seconds, during a grand total of two hundred hours of watching, a beeper beeped in her ear and for the next five seconds Als checked off on her list what she had just observed.

A year later, besides being able to determine within one-second accuracy when fifteen seconds were up, Als knew an enormous amount about how infants and mothers negotiate feeding encounters. For example, mothers tend to look almost continuously at their babies, but they are much more likely to smile and talk when the babies' eyes are open than when they are closed. Also, each mother approaches the feeding with her own individual style. Some love to talk and sing; others remain silent, but playfully tap out a rhythm on their baby's arm. Some respond to baby's every burp and hiccough; others rarely do, but react to each of their baby's fleeting newborn smiles. Babies bring their own styles to the encounter too. Some, like Matthew, respond sensitively to sound, calming readily when they hear a voice. Others seem partial to visual events or to tactile sensations. When a particular mother and baby interact, what transpires between them is individualized by these personal styles.

In the case of Als's research, such results are consistent with what parents may also have noticed. People who have had many children know already that some babies comple-ment their own temperaments, while others challenge their every effort.

Corroboration of parental wisdom is valuable, but research does not always yield, as Als's did, results consistent with what parents believe they are doing when they interact with their baby. Our favorite example of unexpected results from feeding encounters is a study done by Kenneth Kaye and T. Berry Brazelton at Harvard. They selected just one aspect of what happens during feeding: the relationship between the infant's sucking pattern and the mother's tendency to jiggle the baby or the bottle. Babies pattern their sucking into rhythmic sequences: first they make a number of sucks called a burst; then they pause. Nursing mothers often jiggle their babies during the pause; bottle-feeding care-givers may jiggle the nipple as well.

When asked why they jiggle, adults typically volunteer that they are trying "to wake the baby up," or "to get the baby going again." Kaye and Brazelton's videotapes of feedings suggest a very different motivation. Mothers' jiggles did not speed up the feeding; rather, babies paused even longer after a jiggle than during pauses in which they were left alone. In other words, jiggling prolongs the feeding period instead of shortening it. Such a result appears paradoxical from a strictly physiological viewpoint: mothers use more energy to get their babies to take less milk during a given time period.

This finding became plausible, however, when Kaye and Brazelton looked at what happens during a typical jiggle pause. It is not an empty pause. It is brimming over with a communicative interchange between the mother and the baby. The mother turns to look directly at her baby; she may also smile, vocalize, stroke the baby's face or body. The baby, even when two days old, may gaze at her mother's face, relax her arms and hands, and soften her facial expression. Sucking pauses are, in effect, interludes of socializing.

Feeding is apparently not, then, the only purpose of a feeding episode. Communication is another goal, so important it may even override the first so that the efficiency of feeding itself is decreased. Socializing occurs even when the parent (and most surely the baby) is unaware that it is a goal. Yet, although it may be a hidden activity until revealed by the researcher's videotape, it is nonetheless critically significant to both partners.

This conclusion can lead us to reinterpret some other common findings. For example, many parents acknowledge that they spend a lot more time taking care of their first baby than of subsequent ones. Research has backed up that impression: when Evelyn Thoman studied feeding at the University of Connecticut she found that first-time mothers spent much longer (twelve minutes longer on the average) feeding their newborns than did either nurses or mothers who had experience with a previous child. Thoman and others suggested that some new mothers need educating on the fine art of feeding so that they can perform more efficiently. But when we consider Kaye and Brazelton's work, a different possibility comes to mind. Perhaps most first-time mothers are not really being less effective. They may not feed as fast, but they may be spending valuable time learning how their babies communicate. These mothers need not only to become acquainted with this particular baby but also with what babies in general are all about. They need to learn how to decipher baby messages. The best teacher may be the baby, not another adult. And the best occasion may be the feeding situation, with its expansive goals of both care-giving and communication.

In the following chapters we will try to decipher babies' messages about how they feel and think about their first experiences. We will attempt to describe an infant's capacities, and to suggest how these provide the basis for astonishing accomplishments during early infancy. We hope that this interpretation, carefully formulated with the help of the many babies we and other researchers have consulted, will help you gain further insight into who your baby is, and contribute to the excitement of your first months together.

2. Your Baby's Heritage

Before your baby is born, you have already devoted many hours to his care. Not only must you set the stage for his entrance by readying his physical surroundings; you also have a lot of "mental work" to do. You ponder the enormity of what is about to happen to your life. You find yourself increasingly absorbed in concerns about the birth itself and you will almost certainly marvel at how long a task you are about to undertake.

Human parents are well aware that raising their offspring is measured not in months but in years. Compared to most other mammals, our infants are noticeably immature at birth and remarkably slow to develop. Compared to the life cycles of other mammals, ours looks like an elastic stretched to an unbelievable length with the longest segment spanning our infancy and childhood. We do not even expect our babies to toddle much before their first birthdays. Yet baby elephants and goats can run with their herds hours after birth. The almost two-ton whale calf must swim immediately after birth or she will drown in her watery delivery room. Even our primate relative, the chimp, gets around without a parent's aid months before human infants do.

Why does it take us so very long to grow up? Why do we hold the dubious-sounding distinction of being one of the world's slowest-maturing creatures?

Undoubtedly our brains are to blame. Although our baby's brain at birth is enormous in relation to her body size, it is only half the size it will become. The surface of a baby's brain, which at maturity will be convoluted into a landscape of ridges and valleys, will remain quite smooth until the child's third or fourth year. Even the most crucial physiological development, the growth of connections between brain cells, will require several years. And the insulating myeline membrane that surrounds these nerve cells will not be altogether completed until adulthood. But time pays off: although our infants plod along like tortoises in their race toward maturity, when they finally finish, they win hands down (or feet first) over any hare in terms of their stunning cognitive accomplishments.

Yet we are not only incredible thinkers. We are also the world's most amazing social beings. Slow as physical and cognitive development may be, social development will take even longer. As we look into our newborn baby's future, we are intensely aware that nearly two decades of close attention will go into introducing this new human to the complexities of human society.

Adults and the cultures they live in are equipped for this long-term investment. And so are our babies. Contemporary researchers have made scores of novel observations to support the image of a competent, communicative, baby human, who arrives quite ready to engage us in his care and education. Yet these same observations suggest that, in many ways, newborn infants are really not so brand-new. The way they are now is deeply rooted in the past. Each baby enters our world specially equipped for a cultural legacy he or she shares with all human beings, some of whom lived almost 50,000 years ago. Moreover, every infant's history extends back through the many millions of years our species was evolving. We must come to terms with this extremely lengthy past if we are to appreciate the full meaning of our present view of babies.

Although our past leads us to live a uniquely human present, we are shaped by evolutionary processes common to all forms of life. As is true for every species of plant and animal, we do not just live in our world; we are deeply embedded within it. Every change—as slight as a decade of cooler weather, as dramatic as the drifting of whole continents, or as subtle as the gradual penetration of a competitor into a personal environmental niche—poses survival problems. Over many generations, each species must evolve new strategies, both physical structures and behavioral capacities, if it is to survive the challenge of relentless change.

This surviving is no simple matter. It involves a most complex evolutionary problem-solving process in which, over the span of several generations, species change so that they can provide answers to the questions raised by their ever-changing surroundings. These answers are really only tentative "guesses" and, of course, even guesses that are initially correct may not remain so as the demands of the world continue to change. When a species is unable to revise its strategies of adaptation quickly enough, its failure may prove fatal. The past is filled with extinct species, including our own close relatives, which can speak to us only through fossil records.

These records hold clues about who we are as a species since they report at least part of how our ancestors developed strategies that opened the way for our own life-styles. We can and do get some hints from our close living relatives. But even the nearest, the chimpanzee, is more distant than the fossils of our forebears, for, although we share with the chimp almost identical protein structures, we have lived very different lives ever since our last common ancestor became extinct, probably ten to fifteen million years ago. In that far-distant time, the forebears of today's chimps began to meet their own environment's demands with a number of adaptive strategies we never developed, while our own family of ancestors, the Hominidae, struck out on an independent course—the unique evolutionary path that has led to us.

The endpoint of this path, the way we live now, indicates that a very significant part of the route has to do with how we evolved our human way of having and caring for babies. Among countless strategies to assure successful reproduction, many species have evolved complicated methods that involve adult nurturing of immature and dependent offspring. But we humans came up with a truly unique variation on this theme, a social solution of unprecedented scope.

Our story begins with *Ramapithecus,* the first fossil of a hominid that seems to be on its way to becoming human. Though he has been rather stingy with his fossils, willing us only a few ten-to-fourteen-million-year-old jawbones and teeth found in what were then forests in Africa and India, these leave little doubt that *Rama* was a creature more humanlike than any known ape.

Rama's mouth is most intriguing for what it says about his legs. No animal who walks on four limbs has such a curved and arched palate, or such uniformly sized teeth. His students have therefore concluded that *Rama* literally took his first steps toward humanness by standing upright and taking at least a short walk.

About five million more years elapsed before another relative, *Australopithecus,* bequeathed us fossils that suggest how these first steps on two feet affected our evolution. This is a vast fossil fortune, rich with golden hints about how walking creatures might behave. *Austra* definitely walked along with an upright posture, although he probably lacked our grace. Leg and pelvic bones, and even some three-and-a-half-million-year-old footprints are evidence of his gait.

Assured by recent archaeological studies confirming his bipedalism, we can now speculate on *Austra*'s other great strides. Arms and hands that were once used primarily to get around in trees were now grasping objects that could be held and thrown; they were even altering these objects by transforming them into very simple tools. Using these tools, *Austra* began to hunt for meat. And with his new stride, carrying his newly constructed tools, *Austra* left the forest behind, walked onto treeless plains—and into a new evolutionary niche. One seemingly minor change in behavior, bipedalism, thus produced an avalanche of changes; changes that—since five million years separated *Rama*'s first steps from *Austra*'s comfortable walk—proceeded at a rate closer to a glacier's pace.

Austra was not yet fully human. While his brain was larger than those of his predecessors, it was small compared to ours. Yet his advances must have prompted the development of cognitive capacities that would let him make even more effective use of his new gains, for the trend toward a larger brain is as clear in the fossil records of his descendants as are their increasingly narrow hip structure and the gradual appearance of uniquely human hands.

Homo erectus, the next relative in our story and probably the first full-fledged human, looked remarkably like us except for the shape of his face and head. The fossil skulls he left behind over the next several hundred thousand years document the ever-increasing size of his brain. As more modern humans evolved—*Homo babilis* and finally *Homo sapiens*—brain size almost doubled. Although it took about 65,000 generations to get from *Austra* to *Homo sapiens,* this is nothing less than an explosion considering the usual sluggish pace of evolutionary change. Moreover, the shape of the cranial spaces inside those fossil skulls shows that, since *Austra*'s decline about 1 to 1.5 million years ago, the structure of the old arboreal brain was largely revamped. Old portions of the brain, including structures involved primarily in emotional expression and feeling, remained basically intact. Structures dealing with thought developed generously, as regions associated with vision, movement of the hands, language, attention, memory, and planning grew bigger. Through this selective renovation, a new, more complicated brain, one capable of integrating thought and feeling, evolved.

A large brain and the ability to walk bipedally do not, however, end our evolutionary tale or explain our childhoods. Rather, they complicate the plot by posing a unique problem for birthing—how to move a huge brain through a narrow pelvis designed for walking. Human anatomy evolved a few helpful adjustments: a woman's pelvic ligaments loosen slightly before delivery, compensating somewhat for the narrow birth canal required by our erect bodies; and our newborn's head is less bony than other primates' so that it can be molded if need be. Yet these changes are but minor compensations when we consider how large our baby's brain is. This is painfully illustrated today by how we labor to give birth to our young. Our first child usually enters the world only after 14 or more hours of maternal effort; a contemporary ape typically arrives in two. Had evolution not come up with still another answer, our babies could not be born at all.

The central solution we evolved was extremely intricate. Our infants are born extraordinarily immature. If they did not pass through the birth canal when they do, the size of their heads would later make such a journey impossible. But such an early arrival raises certain problems for their hosts. Since our babies' births are but premature separations, they must be allowed to remain almost as close to care-givers—warmed, nourished, cleaned, and protected by them—as they were to their mothers before birth. Who is able to nurture such a needy human being?

The obvious answer is an adult. Someone must take responsibility for each baby and develop a deep bond of caring. But if parents are to devote so much time and energy to the prolonged demands of childrearing, they become increasingly dependent on others. Thus, the investment in childrearing requires a restructuring of all human social relations into a model of intense cooperation and mutual support.

As brain size increased dramatically, as the pelvis narrowed, and as the newborn became increasingly "premature," the need for intense cooperation among adults must have revolutionized our ancestors' existences. Fossils alone, however helpful they may be in reporting the story of our physical evolution, do not document the emergence of the unique form of human parenthood—the exquisite bonding of baby and adult. The human environment, we can imagine, must have become predominantly interpersonal; social systems were revamped to support heightened mutuality. This entailed much more than a mere shuffling and expanding of social roles. Early humans must have had to develop strategies that were not only useful in coping with environmental challenges but could be applied to interpersonal needs as well.

Both emotional and cognitive capacities must have been affected. People needed to be able to work together to develop novel solutions to social problems and to cooperate in implementing these solutions. They also had to evolve strong feelings of empathy so that they cared enough to help one another. And, perhaps most critically, they had to develop communication systems that could let each member know others' ideas and feelings.

Care-giving, cooperation, and communication compose what is called a "cycle of evolution." Gradually our babies' needs increased, as did our capacities for providing for them. Because these needs and our care-giving capacities had to evolve in complementary ways, we cannot separate them from each other, saying that one change caused another. Rather, our special human qualities evolved along a complex spiral course.

Such a cycle of evolution can be viewed from many different perspectives. We can look at the baby and his state of increasing dependency. Or we can view the same phenomenon from the adult's viewpoint. Yet both perspectives must merge, for the baby is, of course, tomorrow's adult. His dependent and immature state puts pressure on adults to cooperate to meet his needs. Interdependency is also a goal of his care, for each baby must develop into an adult who can take part in formulating flexible strategies demanding close cooperation and sophisticated communications. Care-givers must guide the baby not to a state of independence but to one of social interdependence. Though we cannot know the details of how such a cycle developed during the millennia separating *Homo erectus* and modern man, it is clear a new function of childhood emerged.

As much as archaeologists have tried to breathe life into old bones, they can only speculate on what early human social life was like. We may be the last generation to have a chance to guide such speculations with real-life observations of our very first human life-style, the one which man himself has left evidence of in his ancient campsites and recorded in his cave drawings. Today, about thirty small groups of people still pursue a hunting and gathering strategy that was developed by human beings like ourselves perhaps as many as 50,000 years ago. These thirty groups are but a small remainder of the many thousands of similar groups that once populated every continent except Antarctica. They—perhaps only several hundred people—now represent well over 99 percent of all human history. It is doubtful that any of these groups will survive intact into the next century.

Contemporary hunting and gathering societies are far from uniform. The Eskimos of the Arctic Circle, the !Kung of Africa, and the Australian Aborigines must cope with very different environments, which appear to be quite harsh compared to what our ancestors once encountered. Yet all seem to share a similar basic social structure that includes three interdependent units. At the heart of the social structure is its smallest unit, the mother-infant pair. After a baby's birth, he will spend more than three-quarters of his first year with his mother, often in close physical contact. This core unit is embedded within a larger one, a family containing at least a man and a woman who reciprocally share the many tasks entailed in meeting their own and their youngs' survival needs. This family unit is in turn incorporated into an even larger one consisting of many families. As a group, they organize cooperative hunting and gathering expeditions, as well as many other social events, governed by intricate systems of rules.

Although this social structure remains relatively static, an individual hunter-gatherer's place within it does not. He or she must play many different roles—parent, spouse, child, worker—simultaneously. These roles naturally change throughout each individual's life cycle. Each role involves distinct contributions to, as well as expectations from, the group as a whole. Women are primarily gatherers of food; men are primarily hunters. Gathering takes place close to the home and in the company of babies and children, whereas hunting forays may take place many miles from home for days at a time. Within this basic division of labor, there are "specialists" in manufacture, medicine, and other needs. And each contribution, whether in goods or services, is shared among the family unit and the larger group according to clearly defined traditions.

As simple as such a society is, compared to our far more complicated existence, there is no non-human primate culture that resembles it. Other primates neither assign specific food-getting tasks nor typically share the fruits of their gathering. Such division of labor is, moreover, very demanding of social abilities that entail our uniquely human means of communicating with one another.

If all the units of the society are to mesh together smoothly, a lot of time is required to get to know oneself and others. Hunting-gathering peoples take time for this as they engage in the human pursuit of leisure. Far from being continually overwhelmed by pragmatic survival tasks, they enjoy what has been well described as the "original affluent society." Contemporary hunting-gathering peoples spend about half their waking time relaxing together. This leisure time is not wasted time. As they talk, joke, eat, dance, and play together, they foster their cooperation by increasing their knowledge of one another.

In what we must assume to be an ancient, perhaps even a prototypical human society, we can clearly see the outlines of the common cultural heritage our modern newborn babies come ready to assimilate. They, like babies for so many thousands of years, will enter their culture through the door of the family. They will be supported through their prolonged dependency by adults who in turn are supported by the social strategies of their culture. As they learn those strategies themselves—language, reciprocity, and the regulations that govern their people—they will slip smoothly into the workings of the larger group that constitutes their society.

Over fifty years ago, Wolfgang Kohler summarized his famous observations of apes with the statement: "There is no such animal as one chimpanzee." This memorable phrase is even more appropriate to human beings. No human, and especially no newborn human, exists without sharing in our species's social strategies of adaptation. This is the central lesson of our long legacy, stretching from old *Rama* and *Austra* to contemporary hunter-gatherers—and finally to us.

Yet we must exercise extreme caution when we apply

this lesson to our own babies. Because hunting and gathering societies give us such a clear view of our mutual interdependence, it is tempting to conclude that the first life-style our species adopted is the one we either are or should be adopting now. This is wrong. It misinterprets the fundamental trend of our uniquely human evolutionary course.

Millions of years ago, we did develop certain distinctive physical characteristics which still shape our existence. We will probably always look straight with our two feet on the ground, following the lead of our near-human ancestors. And the prolonged immaturity of our children will most likely never cease to place demands on care-giving adults. Yet the evolution of our physical form seems to have ended when our brains reached their current dimensions many hundreds of generations ago. Since then, it has been the capacities of this brain which have directed our evolution along a course marked not by stony fossil records but by the intangibles of cooperation and communication. That course guides us not to a set life plan but toward an open array of diverse and flexible plans, no one more "natural" than the others.

Our evolutionary background poses a unique question to every human infant (and to all care-givers as well): into what cultural form am I born? A mere ten thousand years ago, every baby arrived at essentially the same answer: I am a member of a hunting and gathering society and I will conform to its life plan. Even then, the baby's developmental project had to address a myriad of problems. He would need to capitalize on his human cognitive and emotional capacities to answer certain questions. What is my ecological world like? What skills do I need to develop to fulfill my obligations to my group? What are my group's kinship relationships? What is our verbal language and how do we interpret specific gestures? The questions were endless; the resulting developmental learning tasks monumental.

As cultural evolution proceeded, the newborn's future became increasingly uncertain. By 8000 B.C., some people were living in agricultural communities, and by 3000 B.C., in cities as well. The pace of cultural change, and the increase in cultural diversity, continued unabated. Transformations of

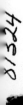

life-style are so common today that we experience "gaps" even between consecutive generations. Today a baby must still come to terms with the cultural "I." What's more, he or she must even be prepared to reevaluate the answer within his or her own lifetime.

Though you and your baby are linked by both the genetic transmission of certain inherited features and by the evolutionary gift of capacities that permit each new baby to experience his group's cultural past, your infant today inherits neither a premade cluster of lifelong behavior patterns nor an inviolate bequest of a preset environment. Rather, babies gain a heritage of flexible social strategies and the capacities to partake of these strategies. They come equipped for communication and participation, and, as they use these abilities, they enter into the stream of the cultural life plan of those caring for them.

Given the diversity of our cultural evolution, we can gain a sense of its processes by comparing life plans in different places as well as in different times. As soon as your baby is born, his or her cultural education begins. Depending on your culturally defined methods of childrearing, you will foster certain of the infant's capacities and deemphasize others.

Consider, for example, how a care-giver in a traditional Japanese family meets her infant's needs:

> The mother cuddles her baby and speaks to him in a slow, lulling monotone. The infant is quiet and still. The mother starts to feed him and he drifts off to sleep. The feeding nevertheless continues. When the infant finally loses hold of the nipple, the mother gently changes his diaper. He fusses briefly and begins to move. His mother holds him in her arms and rocks him. As the baby returns to sleep, she lies down with him and watches him carefully. Gradually he stirs. She pats him and then resumes the feeding. The baby continues to sleep.

This scene is repeated often between this mother and infant;

it is, however, almost never experienced by an American baby. Unlike her Japanese counterpart, the American mother chooses to feed and diaper her infant when he is alert. She concentrates her interactive exchanges within these moments, and she actively encourages her infant to vocalize and to explore the world with her. Sleeping, in contrast, is usually considered an independent activity. After periods of care-providing and play, we put our infants to sleep in their own separate beds, often in their own separate rooms. We may share pleasant cuddles with our drowsy babies, and we often go to them when they fuss in their cribs, but we nevertheless strive to separate solo sleep from interactive alertness.

William Caudill and Helen Weinstein documented these contrasting childcare styles by comparing how Japanese and American middle-class, urban parents interact with their three-to-four-month-old infants. Both groups spend about the same amount of time meeting their infants' biological needs through feeding, diapering, dressing, and touching. But these duties are performed in qualitatively different ways. The Japanese mother soothes her baby, holds him, rocks him, lulls him with her voice. The mother meets her baby's needs at almost the instant he signals them, or even before he is awake enough to signal at all. The American mother is much more likely to "jazz" her baby up, reposition him, "chat" with him, offer him objects. American mothers often seem to set up situations in which they can respond to the infant's signals after, and not before, he communicates his particular desires.

When they are only a few months old, the babies in the two groups already behave differently. To us, a typical infant in a traditional Japanese family might seem overly passive as she sleeps a lot and lies quietly, fussing only occasionally. To a Japanese adult, an American baby probably appears excessively active as she explores her body and her toys, moves her limbs, and vocalizes happily. Yet, to their own care-givers, each baby is acting in a culturally appropriate manner.

Caudill and Weinstein argue persuasively that these care-giver and infant differences are predictably based on what we know about the differences between American and traditional Japanese cultural life plans. They summarize these differences in terms of cooperation and communication: the Japanese are more group-oriented than Americans, while Americans place a higher value on independence. Going along with this, the Japanese appear self-effacing and passive compared to the typically self-assertive American. Our communication styles differ too: the Japanese are more sensitive to many forms of nonverbal communication and make conscious use of gestures and physical proximity, while Americans prefer verbal communication within the context of physical separateness.

These cultural differences are supported by different childrearing methods. Underlying each care-giving routine is a largely unconscious view of who the baby is now and who that baby must become. To the Japanese care-giver, the baby is an independent biological organism who must be encouraged to form interdependent ties with family members and the community in order to develop. The mother, therefore, attempts to establish a symbiotic relationship with her infant, blurring the boundaries between them. In terms of pragmatic details, the Japanese child will sleep and bathe with his or her parents for the first ten years. American methods cluster at the opposite extreme. Right from the start or soon thereafter, our infants are placed in a separate bed and bathed while the parent stands on the outside, vocalizing and positioning. This reflects our underlying philosophy, an image of infants as biologically dependent and of development as a process of individuation. The care-giver acts upon this goal by allowing the infant "space" and by fostering clear boundaries between self and other.

Such diverse cultural life plans, and hundreds more, can coexist because of our evolutionary heritage. Human babies the world over naturally become members of their cultures because they are members of our species. This represents a state of unprecedented evolutionary openness, for it is not until the baby is actually reared—whether among the hunter-gatherers of the Kalahari Desert or in the cultural context of Japan or America—that strategies of adaptation are formed.

Still there are limits to where our cultural evolution might lead. Certainly, not all cultural life plans remain equally viable across generations, as we learn from the current demise of hunting-gathering societies. Further, certain limits will probably never change as long as we are to remain human. Years ago, psychoanalyst Rene Spitz called attention to one such limit when he described how some infants who spent their first year of life in emotionally cold institutions failed to thrive. These babies, adequately if not well cared for in a physical sense, suffered from an acute deficiency of human nurturing. Our very evolutionary openness may make our infants particularly vulnerable to such emotional insults; without the intimate cooperation of adults and the affective exchanges needed to enter into human cultural life, human babies may not survive.

While we may learn enough to outline the limitations of our heritage, we may never have reason to limit techniques to specific childrearing practices. We have no grounds to decide whether bathing with babies or separately, or feeding them at twenty-minute or four-hour intervals, is "best" until we closely consider the cultural context of the activity. The criteria for such an evaluation must be sought in the present social circumstances of the care-giver and infant and the future life they will each pursue.

Similar cautions seem in order when the now familiar debates concerning "who will mind the baby" are aired. Our past certainly does not dictate a specific division of care-giving activities among adults, nor does it prepare a baby to flourish when provided only certain forms of care. Rather, our past allows us to evolve new cultural forms to meet the ever-changing pressures of our interpersonal environment. Our unprecedented social solution to the challenge of our human form is an ongoing one. It has, we hope, prepared us to realize that our human babies are equipped by physical and cultural evolution for interdependency. Interdependency must be respected as the essence of our humanness, and as the basic goal of the adult-baby relationship.

3. Baby
Movements

Would you believe that newborns can walk and crawl? Grasp objects with their fingers and toes? Try to hold onto you if you suddenly let go? Hit or kick the researchers who bother them? Put their hands in their mouths and calm themselves? Even urinate when given the right signal? As farfetched as it may sound, the correct answers are yes. Healthy newborn babies, when examined by a knowledgeable adult, can display talents that many people might otherwise consider more appropriate to the realm of science fiction.

Young infants can perform a whole repertoire of such remarkable feats, many of which have been well documented for some time. Decades ago, in fact, major journals were dense with catalogs of baby movements, and some of these patterns were broken down into component parts and studied with the greatest of care. For example, in the 1890s, Babinski described a seemingly simple response that occurs when you run your fingernail lightly up the outside of a baby's foot from toe to heel. Almost without exception, the baby will immediately spread her toes apart and lift the biggest one upward. By now, this reaction has been studied so thoroughly that we could devote a whole chapter to the eight variations of the response, how the baby reacts differently when awake or asleep, and the way the movement changes as the baby matures.

All this fuss may strike you as obsessive. Indeed, the significance of such specific studies often eludes even "experts." Yet the same concerns that have led researchers to persist in studying baby movement patterns in such detail will probably interest you as you observe some of your baby's actions during his or her first days.

Perhaps the first reason researchers watch babies closely is simply to characterize how they move. It turns out, however, that the very words they choose to describe what they observe greatly influence what they end up studying.

Not so long ago, most baby-watchers placed their observations along a continuum that ran from "reflexes" ("baby behavior is basically a collection of simple, discrete bits of rigidly organized movement") to "mass activity" ("babies typically can do little more than burst into a flurry of aimless activity"). From this perspective, they began to sketch a map of newborn movements that looked either like an intricate network of responses interrupted occasionally by gaps of disorganization or like a sea of random actions punctuated periodically by islands of patterned performance.

These traditional approaches have now fallen into some disfavor. The descriptions they promote are often distorted in two ways. First, regardless of where you place yourself along the continuum, favoring either the rigid reflexes or the aimless bursts of activity, you have already decided to quantify organization in baby movements without considering the quality of the organization. Even if you choose a centrist position—"some reflexes mixed in with some mass activity"— you can easily get caught up in the endless task of dividing dynamic behavior into static snapshots of tiny movements. Second, although the descriptions might seem totally objective, they are not. Lurking not far from the surface are some complicated notions about the neurological basis of baby actions. Concepts such as "reflex" are loaded terms. They often imply that only a portion of a baby's brain can function. If you start out with this restriction, you may eventually overlook or dismiss some amazing observations.

One alternative approach is to begin observations of newborns with the intent of finding an adjective that will describe what is seen. Today's favorite adjective is probably "competent." Babies do so many appropriate things that they leave recent researchers almost awestruck (but certainly not tongue-tied). We endorse this adjective fully, especially since it is such an excellent antidote to previous disparaging characterizations that harped on how much skill newborns lack.

There is another adjective that goes even further in its praise of the baby—"elegant." "Elegant" emphasizes the richness of babies' seemingly simple movements. When newborns coordinate their actions, they often do so with a subtlety that veils their enormous complexity. Rhythm and responsivity (the babies' ability to respond to certain aspects of their environment) are richly meshed in sustained and appropriately directed movements. Moreover, babies often accomp⁻ ;h their aims with such restrained energy that they appear functionally sophisticated.

No better illustration of this subtlety exists than babies' feeding motions. Sucking and rooting are so natural to babies that many nursing women recount how their eager infants taught them how to breastfeed. Even during the first meals, many newborns immediately orchestrate a highly complicated movement pattern with such facility that they make it all look simple.

Appearances can be deceiving. Even a single suck is complicated. An infant does not suck on a nipple the way we adults use a straw. Using his lips and gums, he first seals his mouth around the nipple. After this initial chomp, he then repeats two types of motion. First he "laps." As he presses the nipple between the roof of his mouth and his tongue, and gradually draws his tongue backward, he expresses milk. At the same time, a partial vacuum is created in the front of his mouth under his tongue. Next, he lowers his jaw slightly, drawing the milk into his mouth as it fills the space under his tongue. You can get a feel of the power of this rhythmic alternation of "lapping" and "lowering" by slipping your finger tip into a hungry infant's mouth.

Once milk is coaxed into their mouths, babies must swallow it. They swallow only if what they suck is liquid; otherwise they would fill up on swallowed air. They also mustn't breathe as they swallow, for if they do, they will start to gag. While the "gag reflex" prevents choking, it is hardly a pleasant experience and, fortunately, it is rarely necessary. Sucking, swallowing, and breathing are smoothly integrated. How all this happens is still a mystery, but somehow newborns pace themselves by making about two sucks for every breath.

There is another component of sucking that occurs regularly but still puzzles researchers. Just after babies chomp down on the nipple and ensure that a good seal is made, you may notice that their jaws quiver ever so slightly. No one is sure why babies do this but one interesting hypothesis is that it serves the same function as the more obvious stippling movements of other newborn mammals. Kittens, for example, paw at their mothers' breasts while they suck, and this pawing coaxes the milk down. Maybe our babies' jaw quiver is an understated attempt to do the same thing.

This is already an elaborate sequence: as they feed, our babies seal the nipple, quiver their jaws, lap, lower, swallow, and breathe with hardly an error. Much more, however, also occurs. Before babies chomp on the nipple, they usually display an extraordinary talent for finding it. You can usually get your baby "rooting" by stroking her cheek just before a feeding. As your finger moves, she will track it with an open mouth. The moment you still, she may even catch hold of your finger with her lips, grasp it with a silent chomp, and start sucking. While the accuracy of rooting improves rapidly with practice, even during their first feeding babies can often zero in on a nipple with uncanny speed.

Despite all the evident competence babies display as they root and suck, one might still hesitate to label the sequence "elegant" if babies had to go rigidly through the routine step by step without regard for changing circumstances. Many experiments demonstrate, however, that babies can rapidly modify their sucking pattern to get milk. If they are offered a nipple that works best when it is lapped rather than when suction is applied, they quickly lap more. If they are rewarded with milk only when they turn their heads to the right, they soon pick up on that movement.

Sucking is not rigidly tied to the function of obtaining nourishment, since many objects and even an empty mouth can be sucked. It may be that babies exercise their sucking skills in this way. Babies also spontaneously suck when they start to get fussy. Many well-organized newborns bring their own fists (and even thumbs) into their mouths to enjoy the consolation of sucking. Natural sucking patterns also seem to serve babies well in interactions with care-givers. Human babies are most likely the only ones who routinely start out sucking in bursts separated by pauses. The pauses between bursts, during which care-giver and infant exchange gazes and other expressive actions, are tailored to fit the social nature of human feeding.

Finally, experimenters can get babies to use sucking in ways no rigid inborn program could anticipate. One of the tricks even a two-day-old can master is to turn music on with a burst of sucking. And, if sucking suddenly stops the music, she also can learn to inhibit her sucking. One particularly clever experiment goes even further in demonstrating the ingenuity of sucking infants. Ilze Kalnins and Jerome Bruner once brought one-to-three-month-old babies to Harvard to show them some colorful pictures. The catch was that the babies had to work for the show by coordinating two different and often competing activities, looking and sucking. Some infants had to suck on a pacifier to get the picture in focus and to keep it there; others needed to resist the temptation of the nipple if the picture were to be more than a blur. Even at one month, infants could rise to the challenge and perform complicated adaptive responses. They each gradually developed their own strategy, with some babies altering the burst-pause structure of sucking sequences, others changing their basic sucking patterns into mouthing, and still others coordinating their pattern of sucking with looking away from and toward the picture.

Sucking may well be the most elaborate newborn behavior pattern—and therefore the child's most elegant activity.

But it is also, obviously, a most primitive form of behavior, for it must be ready for action right at birth if the baby is to survive. It is now known that the baby practices sucking for four months in the uterus—one reason she will usually master the coordination involved with a minimum of priming only a few days after birth.

A newborn baby's suck and the appropriateness of this feeding activity are not the only examples of competent, elegant movements. A whole other group of complicated movements, which (once you are aware of them) seem almost as good an example of both competence and elegance, are called "defensive reactions." You can observe how your baby defends herself against potentially annoying events by stimulating her in a number of relatively undisturbing ways. You can, for example, get her to close her eyes by tapping her forehead gently just above the bridge of her nose. If you tap one of her eyebrows instead, she will usually display her ability to localize a touch by shutting only one eye. You can get your baby to perform more elaborate defensive reactions using other simple maneuvers. When you clap your hands next to one of her ears, she will defend two sensory systems—vision and hearing—simultaneously. As she blinks, she is protecting her eyes from potential assault. The rest of the reaction is occurring inside her ears, where the loud noise stimulates her muscles to tighten up and thereby protect the more sensitive parts of the ear from any damage.

Eye-blinking when suddenly confronted with a bright light likewise conceals the full extent of your baby's sensory defense systems. Even shortly after birth, the baby not only blinks when you shine a light toward his eyes, he also contracts his pupils to minimize the amount of light that can enter his lenses. He may even turn his face away from the glare.

Another set of defensive reactions illustrates how vigorous and how surprisingly appropriate a baby's actions can be when he experiences quite disturbing events. You would have to bother your baby more than you want to to see these reactions for yourself, but doctors have noticed them during certain procedures common to the medical assessment of a newborn. First, when a doctor must prick an infant's heel to draw a small amount of blood, the baby does not remain passive. Quick as a blink, he withdraws his foot, often retracting his whole leg all the way from his hip. To examine the integrity of the baby's nervous system a doctor may gently scratch the infant's foot with a blunt needle. The ensuing "cross extensor reflex" is a magnificent example of how appropriately infants can behave. Not only does the baby try to withdraw the foot that is being scratched (the doctor has to hold a baby's leg down to continue to stimulate him) but he also flexes his other leg and then straightens it with remarkable vigor. Some newborns even aim the kick so well that their free foot brushes the needle.

At times, researchers have perhaps gone a bit overboard documenting the amazing abilities of newborns to locate annoying stimuli. For example, when John Watson held a neonate's nose in 1921, he was astonished to find the infant's hand hitting his fingers in less than five seconds; then when he pinched the baby's right knee, the child pushed him away with his left foot. One researcher (who shall remain anonymous) went so far as to attach clothespins to babies. Once again, these unfortunate infants made valiant (but unsuccessful) efforts to rid themselves of such irritating insults.

Certainly needles and clothespins are rare objects in your nursery. But there are other stimuli that elicit your baby's defensive reactions. For example, what happens when your infant is lying down on her stomach and gets her face into the blanket? Without exception, she nuzzles and twists until her nose is free, and, if she has the necessary neck strength, she may even lift her head up a few inches and calmly turn to one side. Or, what happens when a mother nursing her baby presents her nipple in such a way that her full breast presses against her sucking infant's nose? The baby does not interrupt his sucking until he needs to breathe. Then he will arch backward, free his airway long enough for a breather, and lurch forward against the breast to feed again. If this unpleasant state of affairs continues too long, the infant may signal his annoyance to his mother by fussing.

There is one procedure you may not mind performing with your baby if you find these examples unconvincing.

One day when your baby is lookng around while lying on her back or reclining in an infant seat, lightly place a diaper over the infant's eyes and forehead. Hold it ever so lightly at the sides so that it doesn't slip down over her nose. She will most likely protest. First, she will arch her back and start to shift her head from side to side. If you hold the diaper just a moment longer, your baby will probably also start to move her limbs vigorously and apparently without direction. Suddenly, a well-placed swipe may land on your hand or the cloth. More swipes may follow, dislodging the cloth slightly. Some babies get very close to success by swiping, and a few even grasp onto the cloth when they touch it.

It is the cloth that clearly causes your baby's sudden agitation. If you remove it before the child gets overly upset, she will cease moving almost instantly. Some babies calm down so dramatically that they will resume watching the world before you even have a chance to console them with an apology.

Conceivably, although the cloth covers only the baby's forehead and eyes, it could set off defensive reactions against blocked breathing, just as a loud noise sets off the defense of eye-blinking. Or, perhaps the cloth's touch near her eyes is simply irritating. But our experiment using both opaque and transparent cloths, described in chapter one, suggests that blocking the baby's visual exploration of the environment may well provide the cause for the struggle.

Such a clear relationship between a movement pattern and its function is not always apparent when you watch your baby's actions. To try to figure out the reason for baby movements that seem to make no sense, we must take a much broader perspective and speculate on the reaction's probable significance during our evolution. Although we may never gather clear-cut support for such theorizing, speculation can provide some interesting insights into the possible organization of baby movements.

Consider one of your baby's most delightful responses: when you slip your finger into his hand, he will grasp it tightly. Of course, he will hold on to other objects as well, but it is still endearing to "hold hands" with your newborn as you share a feeding or a cuddle. You can also make your baby grasp with his toes by pressing your thumb on his sole. If you watch closely, you can see the intensity of these grasping movements by observing how white your baby's toes or fingers become and how, at least with his hands, he will continue to grasp as you try to release your finger.

The most impressive aspect of baby grasping is its astonishing power. In carefully monitored experiments, infants can even support their own body weight by grasping with their hands. A thin rod is placed across the baby's palms and then jerked upward (more rapidly than a parent would wish to try!). The baby continues to hold on, tightening her grip until she is hanging literally in midair. An Englishman named Robinson was so struck by this feat that, in 1891, he tried to determine how long a baby could swing. He created quite a stir by reporting a record time of two minutes, thirty-five seconds, and by publishing a picture of an infant hanging from a branch.

Robinson was trying to convey, in a none-too-subtle manner, how much he thought our newborn infants owed to their arboreal ancestors. Indeed, baby rhesus monkeys are powerful graspers and can hang from a limb with a single hand for over half an hour. But to appreciate the plausibility of this evolutionary argument, researchers have examined more extensive behavior patterns in which grasping by hands or feet is only one component.

The first of these responses is called a Moro, which superficially resembles an adult's "jump" when startled. At home, it is easy to dismiss this response as a mere startle, since it is most likely to occur when your baby is lying on her back and hears a sudden loud noise. Then, her Moro is so fast that it looks like a mere flurry of fairly disorganized limb movements. Another way of eliciting a Moro reveals its organization more clearly: a specially trained observer holds the baby out before her, one hand under the baby's head and the other supporting his rump. Suddenly the adult removes her hand from beneath the baby's head and lets it drop about four inches before she catches it. This abrupt loss of support and sudden jerk of the neck provokes a dramatic Moro, which, because it is a good indication of the maturity of a prematurely born infant, has been analyzed in minute detail. The younger the baby is, the more he will fling his limbs outward. As the baby reaches the age of full-term birth, the outward thrust of his limbs decreases and is rapidly followed by a full cycling of his arms and legs inward toward his body. His fingers initially extend and then flex into a fist. In the laboratory, the infant usually ends his Moro with his limbs flexed near his trunk, his fists clutching only air, and a fussy grimace on his face.

The second behavior pattern that incorporates grasping is the "placing response." If you brush the top of your baby's foot gently against the bottom of a table edge while you are supporting her upright, she will first bend her knee, withdraw her foot, and spread her toes apart. Then her leg will extend, her foot will flex upward, and her toes will fold inward. It looks as if your baby is trying to step onto the top of the table. With a considerable amount of clever maneuvering, babies can be coaxed to repeat this placing response quickly enough to climb up a set of baby-sized stairs—although their disinterested faces suggest that they have little idea what their bottom part is up to.

In some species, the Moro and the placing response serve more important functions than amusing adults or providing a built-in gauge to the infant's gestational age. A rhesus monkey and a baboon have to be ready from birth to cling to a mother who needs all four limbs to move about. A baby chimpanzee must also be able to hang on to his mother's fur should she make a quick movement when holding the infant against her chest with only one arm. For them, the Moro reflex prevents a bad fall when the ride gets rough. The placing reflex also promotes the infant's safety. Should a branch stimulate the top of their prehensile foot, the response ensures that the baby will lift the foot over the branch and grasp it firmly.

For our infants, Moros and placing responses are probably just remnants of a distant past. Yet there are instances when these remnants may still serve an adaptive function as our babies interact with their care-givers. One clear example was observed in the Kalahari Desert, when a hunter-gatherer mother stumbled and lurched forward while walking with her baby against her chest. The baby also began to fall, and as her head jerked backward she performed a full Moro. As her arms moved inward, her hands touched her mother's beads and closed tightly. In only a moment's time, the infant had become a compact "package" with her limbs tucked in against her mother's body and her hands clinging eagerly. Not only was she now easier to hold, she was holding on eagerly.

We rarely, however, rely on our infants' relatively unimpressive ability to cling. Rather, we have evolved an ingenious adaptive solution. There must have been some point in our evolution as a species when the burden of transporting an immature baby, unable to hold on effectively, demanded too much from the mother. She had to devise a way to free her hands and cease constant monitoring of her baby. And so, some time during our first days, human beings devised a sling to help care-givers. Perhaps this simple device was the first human technological triumph, on a par with any other tool we have invented, and far more basic and important than the much-lauded wheel. This sling freed the hands and attention of the female adult human population for much of each day for most of their lives. We will never know when the sling was first used, for the skins or bark from which it might have been made are not preserved in our fossil records. But, given the logic of evolution, we can guess that it occurred very early and may have in itself permitted our babies to be born even more immaturely, allowing them more time postnatally to accomplish more brain growth.

Being carried allows the baby to remain with a care-giver and interact with adults for long periods of time. Evolution is not always considerate, however, since our babies can soil these moments by eliminating spontaneously. Yet, in the dim reaches of our past, there was a mammalian ancestor whose survival depended upon much neater elimination habits. These beings cached their babies more than they carried them. Today, the direct inheritors of this way of life are primarily carnivores who must leave their young hidden while they hunt for food. These young are left alone for many hours. Were they to urinate and defecate spontaneously, the odor would be a giveaway to their predators. The adaptive solution that has emerged ties the young's elimination of wastes to maternal command. If you watch a female dog care for her new puppies, you will see that when she returns to her infants, she nuzzles and paws them until they respond, and cleans them up as well. Since they tend not to defecate or urinate spontaneously, some carnivore babies will even perish if their mothers do not stimulate them soon after birth.

Human babies may have retained a bare suggestion of this reflex. It is called a Perez reflex, after Juanico and Perez del Pulgar Marx, who first described it in 1955. Superficially, it resembles the way an adult behaves when jabbed in the small of the back. The examiner balances the newborn in the palm of one hand, belly down, then presses his finger along the baby's spine, moving slowly downward toward his rump. The infant lifts his head and emits a sudden, vigorous cry. Then his rump swings upward and, on occasion, he urinates and defecates. As far as we know, no human beings stress their babies in this way to provoke elimination, and the reflex disappears long before controlled habits are typically expected.

Even a journey back to our very distant relatives cannot provide clear clues for the function of some of our babies' organized behavior patterns. They are nevertheless too intriguing to ignore, even if they leave us pondering the question, "Why?". The first is the "incurvature reflex," which, again superficially, is similar to how an adult moves when poked in the ribs. Hold your baby over your hand, belly down. Then alternately stroke one side of his spine, then the other. Your baby will do the "twist" in time to your touches with a beautiful curving of his body and a series of brisk hip jerks. He will look almost like a little amphibian, rhythmically snaking along. Next, hold him under his arms so that he is facing you. Turn slowly with him from side to side and he will follow your lead, by turning his head and eyes in the direction you are moving, in response to inner ear changes produced by motion.

For a charming but perplexing response, take your baby for a walk. Again, hold him upright under his arms but this time bounce him gently so that his feet touch a hard surface such as a crib mattress. First, he will straighten his legs, supporting some of his own weight. Now, tilt him forward a bit so that his feet glide ever so slightly against the ground. His response will look like a walking motion, for his feet will come up alternately and he will begin to march like a little mechanical toy. Some babies, particularly when they are in a rather vigorous mood, will hike with their parents clear across the bed. The charm is obvious, but what is perplexing is that by about four months of age, your baby will no longer walk for you in this way. Unless you work incredibly hard to elicit his stepping movements, he will stand immobile on his toes.

Your newborn can also crawl, after a fashion. You may notice this when you place her on her stomach for a nap. Before she settles down, she may flex and extend her limbs rhythmically until her head is firmly wedged into the crib's corner. Some researchers think that your baby is seeking tactile contact such as that she felt in the womb when "walls" once touched her head continually. Yet again, by the age of four months, your baby may have difficulty getting to the corner she earlier sought out; instead of organizing her movements to produce forward motion, she may merely stamp her feet ineffectively.

There are even more extraordinary examples of this paradoxical developmental pattern in which a baby appears to possess the rudiments of a skill, but then loses them long before the actual skill develops. Newborns can swim. For many weeks after birth, babies can use their crawl-like movements to scoot around in water. Although they keep their heads submerged, they can inhibit their breathing so as not to ingest water. At the age of six months, however, these same babies will flip over, flay their limbs, and cough up swallowed water. One last example is particularly perplexing. T.G.R. Bower of Scotland recently created a tremendous stir with his evidence that newborn babies can swipe at objects dangled within reach, and actually hit them. To observe this yourself, you must act quickly, for in only a month's time a baby's marksmanship greatly diminishes.

Most of the newborn's behavior patterns do, of course, disappear. Except for those that he keeps exercising and readily adapts to new circumstances, the initial repertoire rapidly fades. It is possible to deliberately exercise some patterns such as newborn walking much like a baby spontaneously exercises his sucking. This can keep his stepping organized and perhaps even hasten the emergence of true toddling. But even when this is demonstrated, we still do not know if his earlier toddling is a result of adults' efforts to keep the initial coordination intact or of the strengthening of the muscles necessary for skillful coordination.

Nevertheless, there is something intriguing about the walking-crawling-swimming-reaching newborn's precocity, for these puzzling early behavior patterns—unlike sucking, which fades never to return—disappear and then return as "true" coordinations. These paradoxical patterns may, then, lead us to a different understanding of baby movements by making us take a fresh look both at baby brains and at adult care-givers.

Researchers hope that by continuing to observe newborn behavior they will begin to understand how human brains function. There is no question that brains undergo remarkable transformations after birth, and it seems plausible that our initial behavior patterns reflect our brains at their very simplest level of development. This expectation has, in fact, long guided researchers as they observe newborns. Yet, until recently, the complexity of a newborn's behavior was not fully appreciated, and so the complexity of the new infant's nervous system was similarly underrated.

The behavior of babies has most often been described in the past as a bundle of reflexes. While this term meant many different things to many different theorists, it typically implied that babies must respond rigidly with localized actions to specific stimuli. Paralleling this view of behavior was an equally naive view of a simple nervous system in which the minimum requirement for a reflex was only three nerves—one to pick up the stimulation, one to innervate the muscles used during the response, and a third to connect the two. Although we know of no such triad of nerves, some behavior patterns—such as the knee's jerk in response to a tap below the kneecap—seem to fit the hypothesis fairly well. For more complicated behavior patterns, such theorists postulated a more elaborate network of nerves that chain together simple reflexes.

The "reflex model" made babies seem prewired to make certain responses, and it deemphasized their flexibility. More important, it usually contained the hidden assumption that only the more primitive parts of the nervous system were needed to account for newborn behavior. Indeed, the classic demonstration of a reflex uses frogs whose spinal cords have been cut just below the brain. This surgery ensures that their brains can do nothing to modify their behavior. Even without a working brain, a "spinal frog" briskly withdraws its foot when it is pricked with a pin. Although the leap from the frog to the human newborn is enormous, some researchers treated the newborn as complicated spinal frogs, claiming that only the lower brain and the spinal nerves function at birth; the "higher" cerebral cortex, the hallmark of our humanness, was viewed as beginning to function only weeks later.

In its heyday many years ago, this model inspired some of the very finest observations of newborn babies. Myrtle McGraw, for one, used it as a guide to her detailed studies of how such complicated behavior patterns as neonatal walking and grasping develop during the first year of life. While her descriptions remain valid today, her reflex model for brain maturation does not. According to that model, the baby only used her lower brain and spinal nerves at birth, and was therefore capable only of reflex actions. Then, over the first months, the cerebral cortex began to work by inhibiting these reflexes. Finally, as the baby produced "voluntary," skillful actions, the cerebral cortex not only inhibited early reflexes, but began to coordinate new actions.

To McGraw's enormous credit, she now points clearly to the flaws in her model. In 1962, she wrote a new introduction to her classic book on human infants. She belittles the business of classifying behavior as being under the dominance of either the cerebral cortex or the lower brain and spinal nerves, and she scorns the whole procedure as a cutting apart of brain functions appropriate to the now-ended "age of scientific cleavages."

Even so, the reflex model still influences contemporary researchers, and so you may still come across claims that your new baby can use only part of her brain. There is a growing literature that soundly refutes this view. McGraw mentions many theoretical insights that have ushered in what she labels the new "age of scientific integration." Now the nervous system is viewed as a totality even at birth: the basic integration between parts will change, but one section, such as the cerebral hemispheres, does not take control away from other parts of the brain as your baby matures.

Empirical evidence supports McGraw's new argument. For example, we now know that anencephalic babies (born with an extremely rare and fatal birth defect characterized by the absence of the brain's cerebral cortex) do not act like other babies. They can perform many of the same movement patterns, but compared to other infants their actions are either exaggerated or only partially expressed. Moreover, they seem unable to regulate their responsivity and, thus, they continually react to every stimulus until they are exhausted. There are other differences also—in their sleep-wake cycles, crying, visual responses, and muscle tone—that demonstrate how these anencephalic babies, who indeed have only part of a brain, are qualitatively unlike babies who are intact.

Such observations suggest that the entire brain is involved in producing and modulating your baby's behavior. Surely much of the system is "wired in" at birth, for without such preparation a human baby might never survive. But since your baby develops so rapidly, this wiring must be far from rigid.

That the newborn's nervous system is integrated and flexible, rather than rigid and only partially functioning, still does not explain the paradox of a stepping movement that disappears long before a baby's first independent step, or of a swipe that becomes less accurate just weeks before reaching and grasping become your baby's favorite games. Perhaps such newborn movement patterns are immature precursors of the later skilled actions they resemble. Maybe, as the earliest patterns disappear, the baby has a chance to develop further control of her musculature so that she can practice separating and integrating the components of the movements she at first mixed together. If this is what is happening, the temporary disappearances of these motor skills are not mere lapses in development; they are very important transitions toward more coordinated actions.

Right now we do not understand baby brains and early movement patterns well enough to know if this explanation is correct. But now that we appreciate the competence and elegance of many of a baby's first movements, and now that we see them as reflecting a very complex nervous system, there is one phenomenon that we can no longer help noticing. No matter what eventually develops from the newborn's batting at a dangling toy or squirming across a crib, the baby is demonstrating a desire to touch the world and move within it. The baby's earliest actions contain a thread of intentionality right from the start.

This thread can be traced forward through periods of development as it becomes more and more intricately woven into the baby's actions. To chart its course, we must look at the baby and care-givers together. Limited by an immature nervous system and muscles, the baby can perform only certain behavior patterns. The baby's care-givers find some of the patterns meaningful long before the baby himself realizes that they are. His care-givers understand, for example, that sucking and rooting help fulfill the infant's desire for nourishment. They can see that certain arm movements look like swipes and that certain leg movements are similar to walking. From this sophisticated vantage point, adults can guide the baby to realize the meaningfulness, the humanness, of such actions.

Adults do more, however, than interpret certain baby desires and actions. They also help the baby accomplish such actions and fulfill such desires. Sometimes our aid is relatively minor. The baby, for example, orchestrates his sucking so beautifully that we only need to offer occasional assistance. But, in other cases, the baby's behavior patterns may be to a large measure our own creation: they may occur only when we set the stage, holding the baby so that her arms are free to move outward, or standing her erect so that her legs can move up and down. Now we are the directors who prompt our babies to perform in ways we adults find so exciting.

The patterns of behavior you can see your baby performing are therefore, in a sense, not "in your baby." They depend on what he can do and on the way you support and interpret his activity. This sharing does not detract from your baby's contribution to his own development. Rather, even in his state of dependency, it highlights his central asset: the ability to utilize his own capabilities, along with the capabilities of the adults around him, to enter our social world as a surprisingly competent participant.

4. Baby Perceptions

One of the most thrilling of all experiences is to gaze into your infant's eyes for the first time. For many new parents, this initial contact assures them that their baby is able to sense them and thus begin a new relationship. For weeks to come, you will barely be able to resist your baby's wide-eyed, alert facial expression, just as you will rarely be able to ignore her cry. You will, moreover, work hard to establish a channel of communication using those baby glances. When you notice even a tentative eye opening, you will change your behavior dramatically. You will lean forward and try to meet your infant's gaze. Then you will attempt to hold your baby's attention with exaggerated grimaces, energetic head movements, and wonderfully expressive verbal garble.

When we are face to face with a baby, we do not question what we see, although our perceptual processes are complex and far from fully understood. For example, we take it for granted that the baby is really the three-dimensional, little person we perceive in front of us. Yet, while we willingly act as if we are important perceptual events for a newborn, we often hesitate to credit the baby with any understanding of our appearance. The moment we begin to reflect, a thousand questions emerge. Does the baby perceive our world or does she sense a different reality? Is her world one of depth and solidarity or one of dreamlike blurs? Does she realize that sounds, sights, smells, touches, and tastes emanate from objects, or might they seem disembodied sensations to her? Does her world have sequences of a past before the present moving into the future, or are all her experiences separate and disjointed in time? Perhaps your questions are much more personal. Simply put, you may find yourself pondering whether it is indeed possible for your baby to really see you, hear you, smell you. And, even if her senses are working, can she appreciate you as one person or do you appear to her as separate sensations? Can she even realize that you are the same being when you are close and when you are far away?

Your doubts are warranted. Perception is no simple matter. Objects and events do not simply radiate their appearance to receptive sense organs. It is up to the perceiver to select what is worth attending to. All the chosen moments of fleeting sensation must be analyzed to construct a coherent view of ever-changing events.

To complicate the process further, sensory stimulation without memories and specific expectations often offers incomplete and even inconsistent information about the world. A common adult experience at a cocktail party illustrates how sophisticated perception is. You may be quite engrossed in conversation, hearing the voices around you—if you are aware of them at all—as a jumbled background of human noise. Yet if your name is spoken amidst the jumble, you instantly shift your attention, selecting this detail from the background babble. Once your attention is on target, you use clues such as the speaker's and listener's facial expressions, tones of voice, and snatches of their conversation to reconstruct the substance of their remarks. Memory and expectation of what each might know or think aids your efforts, too, until—and all this may take mere seconds—you have analyzed and evaluated a subtle perceptual event.

Many students of the newborn have concluded that it is impossible that a baby could be preprogrammed for the sensory world as we know it because, while our sensory world contains many constant properties (e.g., depth, separable objects, and temporal sequences), it is forever changing. Jean Piaget, for one, argues that newborns experience "a chaos of sensory impressions"; at most they can see "a fluid mass without depth . . . traversed by images which interpenetrate or become detached without laws and alternately separate and reunite." These fleeting, totally meaningless sensations will, he claims, only make sense once the baby has observed and manipulated objects for many months—developing depth perception, for instance, only through experiences such as reaching for objects that are in view.

Piaget first presented his ideas about newborn perception in the 1930s. His evidence about early sensation was not extensive, and he was particularly interested in the baby's sensory capacities after he or she could reach for and grasp objects. Over the past twenty years, many researchers have not, however, been satisfied to wait until babies could reach and grasp before trying to understand their sensory capacities. Rather, they have tried to tease answers from babies soon after birth by focusing on behavior even newborns seem able to control. The result of this effort has been gratifying. While we do not yet have a satisfactory theory through which to relate all the new, exciting findings, we do have strong evidence that babies are not confused innocents in a meaningless world. Instead, they seem to be telling us that they possess built-in maps, however different these may be from our adult maps, to guide them during their first perceptual explorations. They are, moreover, particularly well equipped to enjoy the sensory landscapes their parents naturally provide.

This conclusion is based on a profound transformation of our view of newborn capacities. We can no longer be content to claim that infants are less discriminating perceivers than are other human beings, though their perceptions may present to them a world different from our own. Infants do not seem to approach their new world with trepidation;

babies seem, in fact, strikingly eager to perceive. As both parents and researchers have noted, babies show preferences for certain things, especially the sound of human voices, sweet tastes, and sights of moving objects. And, although they will be refining their perceptions for many years to come, they somehow master all the rudiments of perceiving well before they speak or even crawl.

The most delightful way to start considering the specifics of newborn perception is to play a few games. Your own baby can provide you with a basis for talking about infant capacities as you engage her in playful interactions that let her display some of her sensory talents.

"Visual chase" is the first game. Support your baby's head while you are holding her in a sitting position on your lap and then put your face about six inches in front of hers. When you think you have her attention, slowly move your head to one side. Continue to shift even if you do not see her follow immediately. Many newborns will pursue you briefly, and, once in a while, they will even turn their heads and eyes all the way to the side. Don't despair if you cannot elicit this response each time; for a newborn, this is a very difficult feat. In a few weeks, your baby will be able to enter into a much more elaborate chasing game, easily following an object like a bright red ball sideways, up and down, and even in circles. You will then also be able to move the object faster and over a greater distance.

The second game can be called "sound chase." Hold your baby out in front of you with her face oriented toward the ceiling so that she cannot see you. Talk to her softly. Watch how she perks up and turns her eyes and head toward you. Some babies even latch onto your face with their eyes once they zero in on where the sound is coming from. This game can be easily turned into a contest between two adults. Should you both try to coax the baby in opposite directions, you may find that she turns more frequently to one of you. We would place our bet on her orienting toward the adult with the highest-pitched voice.

Our final game is "anti-chase." As babies look around, they not only watch interesting events, they also look away from sights that seem to displease them. Demonstrate this by placing your hand or a small pillow an inch or two from your baby's eyes. If she has just been enjoying looking, she will probably quickly turn her eyes from the obstacle and start to stare off to the side. If you then continue to move your barrier into her line of vision, she will continue her escape tactics.

We have observed that, while newborns can play this game relatively well, six-week-olds are true masters. They employ a whole repertoire of strategies. Not only can they shift their heads and eyes away with great speed; they can also regulate how much they take in visually when they cannot avoid the barrier. For example, some babies systematically widen their eyes when they are able to see beyond the barrier, but as soon as it reenters their visual field, they narrow their eyes, or lower their eyelids and look downward. When they face the obstacle straight on, they may even shut it out completely by yawning broadly.

These games are fairly contrived events for your baby. But once you are aware that he can play them, you will notice that he does so regularly without any manipulation on your part. His visual and sound chases occur spontaneously as he reacts to changes in his sensory environment. You may even notice that your baby "anti-chases" if overloaded by too many new and stressful events. The most dramatic instance of such shutting down involves a complete tuning out: the baby suddenly appears to be asleep. His eyelids droop heavily, his limbs relax, and his breathing becomes regular and deep. In a wink, when the overloading events are gone, he becomes alert and begins another journey into the sensory world.

You may be tempted to conclude from these games that your baby can indeed see and hear you. Such basic capacities must be present or else the games simply would never begin. Perhaps you are also now convinced that your baby wants to see and hear you. After all, there are no rewards for the infant in your games beyond getting a glimpse of you and trying to prolong sensory contact with you. In addition, you may be impressed by how absorbed in the games your baby becomes. She doesn't seem to respond mechanically or confine her participation to head and eye movements. You can read her delight or displeasure from her total expression as she brightens her face or grimaces, moves her limbs smoothly or jerks them in agitation.

Your observations may even lead you to some very complicated claims about how your baby organizes his perceptual world. In all the games, he seems able to locate an object in space with an impressive degree of accuracy. His very different responses to visual chase and anti-chase demonstrate that this localization is selective, for he seems able to avoid as well as to approach an object. Finally, you might now want to argue that vision and hearing are interrelated. How else would sound chase be possible? Doesn't this mean that a baby lives in a unified world where sounds lead him to expect certain sights?

Researchers are now taking such games very seriously. Their thoughts about them are not very different from yours. But, they tend to be painfully cautious when they interpret a baby's behavior, and justifiably so. Each possible interpretation involves some enormously complicated capacities. To specify these capacities, very detailed and controlled observations are needed so that we can be sure that other explanations—hypotheses ruling out our claims that babies are indeed rather sophisticated perceptual beings—are not actually the most appropriate.

Of all our senses, the study of sight has attracted researchers the most. Not only is it the adult's most prized perceptual system; it may well be our most complicated.

The most logical place to begin exploring baby vision is to examine the newborn's eye. Actually, this has not proved to be a favorite pursuit, so we are really not very certain about what the baby's visual equipment looks like. The few studies we have, however, do reassure us that our behavioral investigations are not in vain, for the basic visual apparatus is well formed and relatively intact at birth. We have also learned that an infant's lenses are more spherical than an adult's, and that, compared to our flexible ones, a baby's are "frozen" into one shape. This has led researchers to conclude that newborns are nearsighted and often see objects as blurred.

Before we can be sure, however, we have to find out if babies have ways to compensate for their immature lenses.

Finding out how clearly a baby sees turns out to be a true test of an experimenter's ingenuity. When you want to know how clearly an adult sees, you simply ask what he can make out on a standardized eye chart. Of course, we are forced to devise much more indirect probes when we confront a newborn baby. Two such assessments have been developed to exploit a newborn's rather limited response capabilities.

In one baby eye exam, infants are shown two pictures. One is always blank and the other is striped. Babies will look longer at the lines unless they are less than an eighth of an inch thick, and then they seem to have no preference. So, we can be confident that, until this thickness, they can see that the lines are not equivalent to a blank. The second baby vision assessment leads to a similar conclusion even though a different procedure is followed. The newborn watches a slowly spinning striped drum. An alert baby usually fixes on one line and follows it to the edge of her visual field. When she loses sight of it, she jerks her eyes back to the midline and starts to follow another stripe. She can only make this response when she can make out the lines, so we can test the limit of her visual acuity by systematically using drums with narrower and narrower lines. Babies usually stop responding when the lines are about 0.06 of an inch wide.

It is useful to translate the findings of these two examinations into the familiar Snellen notations (20/20 vision) so that we can compare adults and babies. When this is done, newborns get a rating in the neighborhood of 20/150 to 20/670. They improve rapidly, however, and by the age of two or three months they can see as well as most adults.

But we have not completely solved the problem of visual acuity in babies. We have to be careful, since we are relying on how babies answer indirect questions indirectly. In the spinning drum experiment, we expect them not only to make out the lines but also to track them as they move across their visual field. In the preference test, we are making the unverifiable assumption that when babies do not prefer the lines, they do so because they cannot see them. Maybe they can but find them so thin that they like them no better than they do a blank.

Visual acuity is but one of the many aspects of "good eyesight." No matter how sharp an image you can form, all is still a blur if you cannot steadily fixate an object. Part of this steady fixation involves adjusting your lenses to distance. You can almost sense this "accommodation" process by moving your finger back and forth in front of your nose. Notice how rapidly and smoothly you keep your finger in focus. It blurs only when it almost reaches your nose or when you consciously try to stare at the background instead of following its movement.

It turns out to be very difficult to test a newborn's ability to make such accommodations. The most accepted estimate is that newborns can really focus well only when objects are about eight inches from their eyes. Before or beyond this, the world is blurry. By two months, the accommodative system seems to "thaw" and the lenses become more flexible; by three months the lenses work as well as an adult's. Many researchers are dissatisfied with the way these findings are derived. They argue that we have yet to create an accurate test of newborns' abilities to adjust their vision to distance. Yet if new babies have to be content to see objects clearly in only one place, eight inches is an excellent spot: this is just the distance care-givers naturally zoom in to when they try to attract a baby's attention; it is also the usual distance separating a nursing mother's face from her infant's.

Another prerequisite of good vision is coordinating the movement of both eyes. Again, your finger can illustrate how well your eyes work together. Hold it about six inches from your nose and look at it first with one eye, then with the other. Your finger will appear to be in one location for one eye but in another location when viewed with the other eye. You can make the finger seem to settle into one spot by opening both eyes simultaneously. Both your eyes converge on your finger so that you automatically merge the two separate images.

The literature is filled with conflicting statements concerning when babies first get visual convergence under control. Estimates for the onset of this most basic ability run from twenty hours to four weeks to well over two months! The dispute hinges on how you define convergence. Newborns can direct both their eyes toward the same spot. But they are also prone to let their eyes wander independently. Attentive adults are often startled by how often newborns cross their eyes or move one off to the side just when it seems the infants are trying their hardest to look at a special object, such as a face.

So far, we have just scratched the surface of what it means to control the eyes. Human eyes are never still. They dart rapidly around, picking up new images every several hundred milliseconds. Three expert baby-watchers, Marshall Haith, William Kessen, and Philip Salapatek, deserve an award for their patient attempts to track down the activity of a newborn's eyes. From pictures of corneal reflections taken with a complicated infrared television system, they traced what baby eyes do moment by moment in the course of inspecting lines and triangles. After years of work, they ended up with four simple but very revealing rules that summarize the movements of a newborn's eyes.

Rule one tells the newborn, "Open your eyes if you are alert and keep them open if the light is not too bright." This may sound trivial. Yet it is a good warning to all researchers who might otherwise expect babies to perform their visual best in the light of a typical brightly lit nursery. The second rule—"If it is dark, search for the light"—also sounds obvious, but it is truly a profound observation. Babies do not seem to need an outside reason to scan their world. Apparently they are internally motivated to seek out something to see, and so they scan broadly even when the room is totally dark.

Rules three and four direct the baby once he opens his eyes and discovers moderately lit surroundings. Rule three is, "continue your search until you find an edge, a contrast between light and dark." Having hit upon this edge, the infant then tries to "stay near the edge and move your eyes back and forth."

Thus, when a baby first opens his eyes during one of

Haith and colleagues' experiments, he looks around until he finds a black triangle on the white surface before him. Then his eye movements immediately become much smaller and he sticks to just one portion of the triangle's edge without searching much farther. A slightly older infant usually won't get into such a visual rut; he will move on to other parts of the triangle after inspecting one edge. In other words, a baby seems first content to sense mere light/dark contrast, but later he gets interested in the object's entire form.

These four rules were formulated in a laboratory, but we can see their application in the everyday world as well. You may notice, for example, that your baby tends to favor light from a window and averts his gaze from the glare of your flashcubes. Moreover, you may initially get the feeling that, while your baby looks toward you, he zeroes in on your hairline or chin, not your eyes or mouth. By two months of age, however, your baby suddenly begins to explore your features, making direct eye-to-eye contact smoothly and frequently. This change in how you experience your baby's approach to your face coincides nicely with Haith's data on the transformation of baby scanning rules, a transformation from contentment with one area of contrast to an interest in overall form and features.

We are not yet finished describing the intricacies of how human eyes seek out visual objects. Eyes do not make their journeys alone; the head actively participates in shifting their direction. "Visual chase" and "anti-chase" convincingly demonstrate that this integration is not beyond the capabilities of a young baby. Using electronic recording equipment, it is possible to trace both the baby's eye and head movements and then to combine this information to determine the baby's exact line of sight. We have found that infants as young as three weeks of age have better control over where they are looking when, instead of limiting their movements by laying their heads in the depression of a contoured pillow, we allow them to move their heads as well as their eyes.

In other words, your baby can make some fairly complicated eye and head coordinations. If she is fixating on an object, she can compensate for a slight eye movement with a slight head turn in the opposite direction. Or, if she tries to look from one object to another and her eyes move a bit too far, her head will move to compensate for her error. Her head and eyes perform better together than either does alone, and the coordination gives her quite impressive control over her line of sight. At first, the range of this coordination is rather limited because, as Haith and his colleagues found, young babies scan fairly limited portions of the visual field. But by about three months of age, she will be sweeping her head and eyes around, picking up many events in her world.

The baby's initial limitations can be observed in another of our investigations. Even when you look straight ahead, you sense what is happening off to the side. People from four months of age through adulthood usually will notice an object as much as ninety degrees off center from their direct line of sight. Thus, if you were to hold your finger about twelve inches out from your ear, you would see it even if you focused directly on this page. Newborn babies probably would not. At first their peripheral vision is limited to a total range of about fifteen to twenty degrees. When an attractive object is placed outside this limit, they do not shift their gaze toward it to get a better look. The available visual field is also probably not very deep for the newborn. For whatever reason—blurriness or some as yet unknown factor—most things that happen more than a meter or two away from newborns receive little notice. In contrast, two-and-a-half-month-olds may spend minutes watching events occurring across the room. There may also be a temporal constraint: it now appears that babies need much more time than do adults to process each sensory impression; thus, newborns cannot take in rapidly occurring events.

All these detailed observations of the baby's visual equipment indicate that newborns are able to see objects and to control where they look. They have to overcome some initial limitations, but they seem to do so quite rapidly. And perhaps those limitations are at first even necessary to spare newborns from overindulging during their first sensory feasts. Built-in constraints that keep certain portions of the perceptual world off-limits to very young human beings might conceivably help them deal with those portions of the visual diet that are available to them. Before these limitations were uncovered, it was very hard for researchers to know what infants could see. Babies who failed to respond to fast-moving events on the other side of the room might mistakenly have been considered to possess meager perceptual capabilities. Before it was noticed that newborns needed the help of head movements to track objects with their eyes, contoured pillows restricting such movements made babies appear less visually able than they actually were. Another mistake was to test babies when they were lying on their backs. It is now clear that babies are most fully alert when they are in more upright positions. Parents seem to have known this all along, for they often seat their infants or hold them against their shoulders when they interact.

Considering both the limitations we have observed and the conditions of freedom of movement and upright position that show a newborn's abilities at their best, we could now perhaps design a super-object that would prove very attractive to the newborn. This object would need to be relatively large and be placed not too far from the baby's eyes or line of sight. It might be most interesting if it moved, but since the newborn would not be able to process visual information about transformations very rapidly, it should not move too fast. It would also help if the object had distinct contours, or edges, and areas of strong contrast between light and dark.

Our adult faces naturally conform to these design requirements for a super-object. They are filled with features, like eyebrows and noses, that are sharply contoured and detailed yet are still quite large. Moreover, they constantly turn up in just the right place for the newborn's eyes—eight inches away and straight ahead. And because our faces do move, they are even more attractive. Adults modify their facial expressions when they address a new baby. These modifications are beautifully tailored to the baby's visual system. We smile slowly and hold our grins for many seconds; we exaggerate our usual facial movements (widened eyes, arched and raised eyebrows, and flashing teeth) accentuating light/dark contrasts. Our faces bob and weave slowly, often remarkably in tune with the infant's line of sight and ability to shift his gaze.

Despite how well our faces complement the newborn's visual abilities, researchers are having a hard time figuring out how a face looks to a baby. Constructing such a portrait involves inferring what babies see when they look based on how they look when they see. Our probes into this covert world are limited by what babies can do at birth. We can never be really sure that they are not hiding quite mature (or quite amazing) perceptions behind a facade of immature overt actions.

One of the most popular techniques used to investigate a young baby's covert perceptions is called the "preference method." Parents had long noticed that their babies gaze at such visual events as the pattern of dark and light produced by venetian blinds. These parents had no trouble claiming their baby "liked" such sights. Researchers, however, seemed to discount the notion that infants could select certain sights, thus showing a preference for them. By 1956, when Robert Fantz of Case Western Reserve University fathered the preference method, the time was ripe for researchers to finally believe their eyes and to exploit babies' natural ability to look selectively at certain parts of the world. Fantz systematically controlled what babies could see, presenting them with two pictures that differed by only one property. If the infants consistently looked at one picture longer than at the other, Fantz argued cogently that they revealed that they can perceive the property.

Hundreds of studies, including the one that helped to probe how clearly babies see when the varied property is line thickness, have been based on this simple design. From these studies, we have learned much about how babies first perceive the world. They seem to be able to tell the difference between light intensities, preferring moderate intensities to either very bright or very dim ones. They differentiate between colors and, at least by four months of age, they group them as we do, preferring pure colors such as red to "boundary" colors such as red-orange. Moreover, they usually prefer patterns over solids, objects in motion over static ones, and moderately complicated drawings over either very detailed or extremely simple pictures. All their favorite properties fit quite well with what we have learned about the sensitivity and limitations of the newborn's visual apparatus.

But what about the human face? Do newborns show us that they see it as we do and that they prefer it over other objects? We have no straight answer, not because researchers have not been trying to provide one, but because faces possess so many properties at once. Like most objects in the world, our faces do not differ from other objects in a simple way. It has been impossible, in fact, to come up with suitable preference-method options that neatly break down our complex physiognomies into distinct properties.

In many early studies, experimenters tried to define faces by reducing them to their critical elements. The typical solution was to use an oval with two dots for eyes and with one or more lines to suggest the other facial features. To an adult this symbolizes "face," but to a newborn it may very well not. Baby preference behavior does not tell us for sure. When the schematic face drawing is paired with other pictures—a concentric-circles bull's eye, an oval with "scrambled" features, and newsprint—very young babies rarely look at the "face" for much longer than they study whatever is paired with it if both contain a similar amount of contour or degree of overall complexity. The more the researchers persisted, the more tangled the babies' replies became. All too often babies in one study selected one picture while their peers in another laboratory preferred another.

Two recent changes in the preference test may help us develop a more clear-cut answer to how babies view human faces. Fantz's classical test allowed the babies to express preferences only by moving their eyes. Now the babies are often allowed to make more complicated responses which include turning their heads. Carolyn Goren and her associates showed newborns, immediately after delivery, a series of standard pictures drawn on squares—the schematic face, a scrambled version, and a blank square—and the researchers moved each in a visual chase game. The babies were more likely to fixate on and follow the schematic face than the other pictures. Many minute-old infants even turned a full 180 degrees just to keep looking at the most humanlike drawing. In effect, then, they displayed a preference for the human face before they had actually ever seen a real human face (unadorned by a delivery-room mask). Goren argues that the babies demonstrated an innate ability to distinguish between a face and pictures with an equal number of elements.

The other change in the preference method altered what was used to represent a face. Researchers gradually made the test faces look more like real ones. First, they tried to replace them with photographs, including one of Joan Crawford. Very young babies, however, did not fulfill their fondest expectations. Even Ms. Crawford proved less attractive to the babies than did the schematic faces, perhaps because the actress's photograph did not contain an equivalent amount of sharp contrast. Next, three-dimensional representations of faces, and then real ones, were introduced. Three-dimensional objects often won the baby-looking contest, for babies preferred sculptured faces to flat pictures. But between a pair of three-dimensional objects, the way babies tend to treat faces, especially their mothers', may come as quite a surprise.

Genevieve Carpenter, in a series of carefully designed studies at the Research Unit of St. Mary's Hospital in London, watched babies looking at their mothers' faces, a store mannequin's head, and a kitchen colander with three small sticks protruding to represent two eyes, and a mouth. Each was shown to the baby through a small window. By two weeks of age, the babies were clearly spending differing amounts of time looking at each display. But they were paying the least attention to their mothers! Not that they acted as if they were bored or uninterested; rather, when their mothers' faces appeared in the small window and stared out at them, the babies tensed and tried to avert their gaze. They took very short, furtive peeks at their mothers, but these glances did not add up to a lot of looking. Many infants even cried, so that calculating the total time they spent looking seemed inappropriate.

Given such experiments, it seems that even young babies may understand that a real face is a different sight from other three-dimensional and quasi-facelike objects. But this is not the extent of the babies' sophistication. They are sensitive to the conditions under which they view such faces. Essentially immobile faces appearing in an atypical context (such as an experimenter's window) may provoke fright instead of the increased attention hoped for. Thus, researchers have now been challenged by their complicated newborn subjects to devise more realistic ways of probing the baby's covert experience. And, as they take up this challenge, they may find it near impossible to design experiments that neatly sort the visual world into easily definable properties.

Nonetheless, there have been a few startling new probes that both respect babies' sensitivity to distorted contexts and tell us about how they perceive specific visual properties. Some of these investigate how babies comprehend the effect of movement on object size and location. This raises important questions, since real faces are indeed rarely still in a baby's world. Adults tend to move their faces within babies' visual fields, often nodding and twisting with exaggerated tempos. Can babies comprehend such movements? Do they understand, for example, that as you move farther away your real size does not change? The size of the image that falls on the retina does indeed get smaller as an object moves away from the eye, but adults unconsciously compensate for this apparent change and keep track of the "real size" of the moving object. For a long time, it was assumed that babies learn from experience how to make this conversion from retinal to real size, and that, before they learn, newborns perceive a world in which objects continually balloon up and shrink down.

In 1964, T.G.R. Bower came up with a fascinating way to refute this claim. He began by teaching one-to-three-month-old infants how to play a special game of peek-a-boo. Every time the babies saw a 30cm cube one meter from their eyes and then turned their heads to one side, an adult popped up, all smiles and "boos" to delight them. Babies learned to play this enjoyable game after a little practice. Then Bower cleverly varied the cube's size and location to see if he could trick his babies into playing the game with the wrong cubes. He used the 30cm cube, but at a distance of three meters, a 90cm cube at one meter, and a 90cm cube at three meters. The last cube—three times larger but also three times farther away—provided the babies with exactly the same retinal image as the original 30cm cube at a distance of one meter. Were the babies fooled into turning their heads? Bower thought not. His babies turned their heads four times more often to the "correct" display (the 30cm cube at three meters) than to the cube three times bigger and three times farther away. So, very soon after birth babies seem to be able to make at least some general calculations about real size. We can, then, be a bit more certain that as parents bob closer and farther away, babies are not seeing them expand and deflate.

This means also that babies may be able to comprehend that our perceptual world is a spatial one. To us, objects usually seem to be following predictable courses instead of jumping haphazardly around. Again, Bower and his colleagues came up with a dramatic demonstration of the infants' ability to perceive systematic changes in object position. In this experiment, babies as young as six days old were presented with objects, such as a flat white square or a "virtual" object that was really an experimentally produced shadow. As the object gradually approached them, the babies acted defensively. They widened their eyes, retracted their heads, and even put their hands up between their faces and the approaching object. They certainly seemed to realize that the way an object changed position in space related to their own position. There were some limits, however: since their visual equipment does not register events as rapidly as our eyes do, the babies did not react defensively when objects moved very rapidly.

Babies may nevertheless perform some astonishingly adaptive calculations. We and Bill Ball once complicated Bower's procedure and, in the process, increased our appreciation of babies' comprehension of depth. We showed babies styrofoam cubes that approached them on a course of impending (but, of course, never actual) collision, and documented the babies' appropriate defensive behavior. Then we moved the same object along a diagonal course that to adults suggests the object is nearing but will miss hitting them, and we also made the object move away instead of toward them. Under these conditions, the infants also acted appropriately. They calmly watched the object, and even turned their heads to follow its movement.

Studies like these suggest that babies do begin viewing a world that, at least in its barest outlines, looks like our own. It is too early to say exactly to what extent our worlds are similar and different, but we are now in a position to appreciate that even new babies may share certain basic visual processes with other human beings. This, in turn, makes what adults do with their babies all the more sensible. We adults do not barrage infants with stimulation that totally mismatches their initial capabilities. Rather, even with our faces, we unconsciously feed their visual sense, providing them with the experiences they will need to develop even more adequate visions or perceptions of a most complicated environment.

Most sights in our world are accompanied by sounds, touches, and even tastes and smells. We know less about how babies process these sensations than we do about their visual perceptions. What we have so far learned does, nevertheless, echo our conclusions about baby vision. All baby perceptual systems seem to be functional at birth. Moreover, their senses of hearing, smell, taste, and touch, although perhaps different from adults', seem well tailored to permit new babies to meet their human companions.

Babies' hearing is particularly interesting, for they seem to practice it before they are born. By their fifth month of life in the uterus, baby ears are functional, and by their seventh, they respond differentially to sounds of different intensity, moving more vigorously the louder the sound. Even without noisy researchers adding to the din, intrauterine homes are far from silent. The mother's heartbeat and assorted digestive gurgles continually invade its walls. As many pregnant women come to appreciate, unborn babies also hear nonexperimental outside noises, since they often dance vigorously to loud music and startle to sudden clashes.

All this prebirth experience seems to shape our infants' first reactions to sound. They may, for example, cry less if they hear a heartbeat after birth. As Lee Salk has tried to demonstrate, adults may realize this intuitively, holding their new-borns "close to their hearts" regardless of whether they are left- or right-handed. Evidence indicates that other noises may also be remembered from before birth. For example, babies who spent their prenatal months near Japan's Osaka airport tended to sleep soundly through the roar of a plane flying overhead, while infants who arrived at the hospital from afar rarely did (see p. 101 for more detailed discussion).

To adults, the most critical sounds are those of human speech. Babies too seem attentive to sounds in the human speech range (500-900 cycles per second), and especially to the relatively high-pitched noises that adults emit when they try to amuse or soothe their newborns. This is why, in our game of sound chase, we predicted that your baby will turn most often to the higher-pitched adult voice (which usually belongs to the woman in any contest pitting male against female).

Babies may also be prepared to process the fine nuances of human speech. Peter Eimas of Brown University is now watching how babies change their sucking patterns in response to hearing certain speechlike sounds. They usually pause when they hear a new sound, and continue to suck only if the sound is one they are used to. Eimas is finding that babies can differentiate among many sounds common to speech. Even more surprising, he has evidence to suggest that babies as young as one month react to some of these sounds in the same categorical ways we adults do. Take the sound *ba*. Specialists can characterize a physical property called "voice onset time" for many acoustic signals that all sound like *ba* to us. Another group of signals that has a different range of voice onset times is the sound *pa*. According to Eimas's results, babies indicate their own perception of the difference between these two sounds by pausing in their sucking; they hear *ba* and *pa* just as you do. Within only a few weeks after birth, they are categorizing some of the segmental sound units of speech, already processing spoken language in a linguistically relevant manner, even though they cannot yet produce their own versions of these sounds and even though they have had very little experience listening to human speech.

Babies may perceive other critical human sense experiences as well. They undoubtedly sense our touches, reacting with localized and often appropriately directed movements, such as blinking or rooting, when we tap or stroke their skin. Newborns also seem ready to enjoy our human smells. This is a recent discovery; until a few years ago the smells we presented to newborns in the laboratory were strong scents, such as anise, acetic acid, and phenyl alcohol. Now, thanks to Dr. Aidan Macfarlane, a pediatrician at Radcliffe Infirmary in Oxford, England, we have learned that babies can also rapidly learn to smell their mothers. Right before feeding time, Macfarlane held to one side or another of a baby's cheeks the mothers' milk-soaked breast pads and unused pads. After a minute, he alternated sides. By their fifth day, babies predictably turned to sniff the milky pad. Stimulated by this striking finding, Macfarlane made each baby's task even more challenging. He used two breast pads, one from each infant's own mother and the other donated by an unfamiliar nursing woman. Two-day-olds did not yet display a preference. Six-day-olds spent slightly more time with their noses aimed toward their mothers' pads. And ten-day-olds rapidly made the correct selection, demonstrating that they had learned to smell their mothers' milk.

Macfarlane's work helped to explain a phenomenon that many nursing women lament. Often by three weeks of age their infants noisily refuse to accept supplementary formula from them unless they are extremely hungry. The father or another helpful care-giver often steps in, however, and readily initiates a successful feed. The mothers may be astonished and perhaps a bit annoyed. But they can take heart that whatever the reason for their newborns' refusal to accept bottles from them, their very tiny infants may already be demonstrating recognition of the mothers, based perhaps on the subtle perfume of their milk.

Similar abilities to differentiate between various relevant stimulations have been demonstrated in regard to the newborns' sense of taste. Researchers have found that babies distinguish tastes, and quickly come to prefer tastes such as sugar over salt, quinine water, citric acid. They systematically alter their sucking patterns when they are offered such everyday liquids as orange juice, formula, or sugar water. Intriguingly, the pauses in their natural burst-pause-burst sucking pattern are most lengthy when they are drinking breast milk.

Discussing each sense separately is a sufficient challenge in today's research world. Yet, as our appreciation of newborns grows, so does the significance of the question of how they coordinate all the sensory information they register through seeing, hearing, touching, tasting, and smelling. Right now, two views are often pitted against one another. The most established is proposed by Jean Piaget. He argues that the baby first acts as if each sense brings with it a separate world. The baby sees, hears, and so forth, but does not realize that sights can produce sounds or that seen objects are solid and touchable. Gradually, after some experience manipulating the world, the baby develops an understanding that the senses are coordinated.

The other viewpoint is suggested by T.G.R. Bower. He claims that the baby begins with a "primitive unity" of the senses. Sights, sounds, touches and such all blend together. With development, the infant differentiates among the senses and thus achieves a more coordinated and balanced appreciation of sensory stimulation.

A third possibility exists. A baby may, indeed, process sensory information in a way that is not qualitatively different from the adult way. One sense may indeed suggest to the baby that his other senses may be stimulated in a specific way. Thus, if he sees someone moving her lips, he may already expect that the sound he hears emanates from those lips. Or, if he sees an object, he may already expect the object to be solid and, hence, touchable. This viewpoint does not rule out development; rigid, preset expectations would be impossibly unadaptive in a world that is filled with surprises. Yet, at least a general interrelationship and coordination of the baby's senses may already exist at birth so that, as the baby gains experience in sensing, he can refine his initial organization.

It is too early to decide which of these three views is most appropriate. There are some findings—for example, the different reactions babies exhibit when their eyes are covered by opaque or transparent cloths—that suggest that the third view may have the edge right now. Babies felt the same sensation when their eyes were covered with either cloth, but they only reacted with directed defensive movements when their vision was blocked. This is compelling evidence that they can distinguish touch from sight well enough to act appropriately in the two situations.

Another suggestive finding is babies' adaptive "self-defense" of themselves when an object loomed toward them. We can infer that they somehow expected the visually approaching object to have some tactile substance—why else would they have made protective responses when it moved on a "hit" course?

T.G.R. Bower has conducted an experiment that goes even further. He claims that if you visually present a very young baby with an object, he will swipe out at it. But you can trick him, using fancy shadow-casters to create the illusion of a solid object that actually lacks substance. Should the baby's hand intersect this optical illusion, the baby appears surprised and often gets suddenly upset. He acts as if his prediction that seen objects are also touchable objects has been dramatically invalidated.

Babies also seem to react with some distress if you violate their expectation that visual and auditory information is coordinated. We saw the expectation at work as they turned to locate our faces in the game of sound chase. Aronson and Rosenblum, working at Harvard University, attempted to get one-to-two-and-a-half-month-olds to demonstrate an even more sophisticated notion about how sounds and sights are related. Each of the babies first watched and listened to his mother speaking to him from behind a glass barrier. The baby remained calm as his mother's voice emanated from her mouth. Then, the experimenters switched the speaker system so that, while the mother continued to speak and her baby could see her lips move, her voice came from either her left or her right. The babies violently objected to such a subtle dissociation of sound and sight by grimacing, fussing, jerking their arms and crying.

Apparently, young babies can integrate the information they receive through different sensory systems. Coupled with all the exciting research concerning how well each sense functions, we can indulge a view of the baby as an extremely able perceiver. From the start, she is prepared to interact with a world that offers complex stimulation. She does, of course, still have much to learn about the nature of her new world. Yet, she is ready to take advantage of all the initial stimulation she receives, in order to develop adaptive perceptions rapidly.

Since the baby seems to sense one world through many senses, you are, as you offer yourself, offering her one package of reality. You stimulate all her senses. And, you do so sensitively, modifying your presentations to suit her capabilities.

Even though we do not know exactly how a baby first perceives the world, we still must marvel at how well caregivers complement his first sensory abilities. Unlike most objects confronting the baby, adults strive to offer the infant all the ingredients of the sensory feast he must eventually come to digest. We measure out these ingredients—sights, sounds, smells, touches—and sensitively blend them together to provide a balanced diet that suits the baby's current appetite.

Of course, we rarely feel as if we are making an effort to provide the infant with just the right forms of stimulation. Usually our adjustments to the infant's sensory capacities are subtle, unconscious aspects of our interactions with him. Yet, almost every adult-infant interaction illustrates how well we serve our infants. For example, in the following scene, we can observe how Terry continually tailors her activity so that she assists and stimulates her new grandson, Daniel:

> Terry quietly stands next to Daniel's bassinet as he begins to stir at the end of his nap. She watches as his eyes gradually open, and then she leans over so that her face is parallel to his, about a foot away. She then gently wraps Daniel's arms and legs in a receiving blanket while speaking slowly and softly. She periodically punctuates her tune by stroking his forehead in time to the beat of

her speech.

Terry lifts the now-swaddled Daniel smoothly upward and holds him close to her left side, taking care to support his head in her hand. Daniel actively nestles, and then he straightens his body a bit and lifts his head erect. Terry turns and looks at his face, speaking more loudly and with a more elevated pitch than before. After a moment of eye-to-eye gazing, she settles down in a chair and moves Daniel to her lap, helping him maintain a sitting posture. She leans forward, positioning her face just inches before his eyes. As he looks steadily at her, Terry quickens the pace of her singsong and emphasizes the end of each phrase by bobbing her head and making a comically exaggerated face. When his attention momentarily wanes, she strokes his cheek gently and attempts to recapture his gaze by moving into his new line of sight.

Terry helps Daniel perceive a coherent world in many ways. First, she continually sets the stage. She swaddles his limbs gently to contain otherwise disruptive limb movements, and she supports his body and head upright, helping him maintain alertness. She also constantly leans toward him, locating her face just where he is most likely to be looking. Once the stage is set, she entertains him with a perceptual performance. Her show of varied sounds, sights, and touches is suited to her audience's limitations, its overall content bonded by the rhythm of her tune. Finally, she does not act without taking into account what her audience asks for moment by moment; every time Daniel changes his receptivity to sensory stimulation, Terry attempts to alter her own activity to meet his current condition.

Undoubtedly Daniel has a number of very difficult perceptual problems to solve during his first weeks. Yet when he is with a sensitive care-giver, he is not forced to formulate solutions on his own. Although adults have a very different view of the world, we constantly and often unwittingly alter our behavior to provide infants with perceptual displays that match their current abilities and push them gently along their developmental course. The infant perceiver is thus part of a relationship with more sophisticated adult perceivers; it is through complex interactions with adults that the baby comes to understand the perceptual qualities of the sensed objects.

5. Babies as Individuals

A casual visitor to a large well-baby nursery is often impressed by the uniformity of its occupants. At no other point in our life cycle do human beings appear to be such conformists. When else could you observe so many people dressed in identical fashion lying in the same rump-up, tummy-down position? When else will they seem to vary so little in size or in action? It might appear then that newborns possess very few ways to distinguish themselves in a crowd; each one so much resembles the others.

The parents of each of these babies take a much different view of the situation. They have been preparing to meet just one (or at most two or three) of the babies. To them, this infant's appearance and behavior already mark him or her as an individual. Each minor variation in looks or actions generates great interest, for it might reveal unique qualities and potential. Parents most certainly would not accept another baby as a valid substitute! And, because they are so motivated to accept their one infant as unique, they would rarely agree to the casual assertion that any single newborn is an adequate representative of the entire group.

Researchers seem to vacillate between the perspectives of the casual observer and the new parent. In much of their work, they are strongly motivated to issue general statements about all babies. Any variations among newborns are like annoying noises that mask the general processes they are concerned with. They try, therefore, to highlight what the babies have in common, minimizing potentially "noisy" variables such as size, sex, and temperament.

It might seem likely that those researchers who spend their careers trying to achieve control over such variables could lose sight of how each baby begins as a unique individual. Yet, newborn infants rarely allow researchers to hold such self-serving illusions for long. No matter how hard the latter work to standardize a situation, babies just refuse to act in identical ways. Given the rich complexity of newborn behavior, there is plenty of room for individual expression. Thus, during most experiments, the harried researchers are tempted to conclude that their uncooperative newborn subjects assert their individuality in every way possible. After all their data are in, they must spend long hours using statistical tools to shift and slice their findings so that common points are apparent amid the distracting range of variability.

One researcher's misfortune is, however, another researcher's delight. Certain researchers have been attempting to make use of infant individuality to answer some very important questions. They would like to know, for example, why some babies seem disrupted by some minor stress while others are barely affected by the same event. They would also like to develop a better understanding of how human beings vary at birth; they might then be able to predict what the same babies will be like a few weeks, months, or even years later. And they would like to be able to understand how individual babies and individual adults mesh together in their own very personal ways.

Focusing on individual differences has not, however, spared these researchers from some of the same frustrations experienced by colleagues concerned with studying the characteristics babies have in common with one another. They, too, need to formulate a working vocabulary that adequately summarizes their observations. They, too, are constantly trying to tread the fine line between seeing every action as unique and considering all behavior patterns as "typical." After all, even if they ultimately want to develop a theory of how each baby develops as an individual, they cannot do so by spending a lifetime observing only one baby. Somewhere between the richness of specifics and the simplification of generalities, we hope to conceptualize the principles of individual development.

Pediatrician T. Berry Brazelton is perhaps the most influential contemporary champion of the newborn's individuality. He has spoken frequently to care-givers, always emphasizing that there are as many individual variations in how babies behave as there are babies. In his book *Infants and Mothers* he has provided a generation of parents with a compelling way to discuss differences among infants in their early development. In addition, as director of Harvard Medical School's Child Development Unit, Brazelton has alerted his professional colleagues to the critical importance of individuality during the newborn period. With an ever-growing group of admiring collaborators, he has spearheaded a movement toward precise evaluation of each baby's own ways of adapting to our world.

The most popular of Brazelton's scientific contributions is a behavioral examination called the Neonatal Behavioral Assessment Scale. "The Brazelton," as it is commonly referred to, has been used with thousands of newborns in hundreds of settings across the world since Brazelton began to develop it in the 1960s. The test grew out of Brazelton's cogent insights into what makes individual babies and their care-givers tick.

Brazelton's insights can be summarized by three adjectives: *marvelous, dynamic,* and *interactive.* The first probably strikes you as very nonscientific and, indeed, Brazelton probably uses the term in part to shock his medical colleagues into realizing that babies are brilliantly gifted beings. Newborns have rich repertoires of behavior patterns, and organize these patterns in ways that we adults cannot directly control. We do infants a great injustice when we try to disassociate their behavior patterns from their entire constellation of adaptive mechanisms. They all have *marvelous* capacities for actively adapting to events in their new world.

Brazelton also argues that to understand how each baby expresses these marvelous organization capacities, we must watch him in action. A baby is a *dynamic* person. He is always modifying his actions so that we cannot expect him ever to repeat the same action in exactly the same way. Particularly after the stresses of birth, he has to reorganize himself right away, and this entails rapid alteration of his behavioral organization. Thus, if you want to grasp each baby's uniqueness, you must take more than a single look at him and you must study more than one type of response. He expresses his individuality as much in the way he changes as in the way he performs any particular action.

Brazelton's babies are not just *marvelous* and *dynamic*. Such stunning qualities would still not support the immature infant's quest for survival. A third adjective is necessary to convey the newborns' ability to "capture" others who can assist them as they cope with the stresses of reorganization. Brazelton thus argues that babies are *interactive* from the start. They never exist in a vacuum, never behave in isolation from us. Nor do they merely react passively to what we do. Rather, they mobilize their marvelous, dynamic behavioral repertoire to "hook" us into their developmental process.

Creating a formal examination procedure out of these insights was an enormous endeavor. Brazelton and over twenty collaborators from fields as varied as medicine and anthropology spent years documenting how babies differed in their patterns of specific actions, in their styles of regulating their responsivity, and in their methods of hooking adults. Finally, in 1973, a version of "the Brazelton" was published.

The Brazelton manual instructs the examiner to spend about thirty minutes closely observing the baby as she reacts to over twenty-five different maneuvers. Brazelton selected maneuvers reflecting what parents might do naturally as they interact with the baby; the test is a small window through which to view the complexity of a baby's adjustments to a multitude of ordinary events in their postbirth world. Some of the specific behaviors observed include such baby movements as defensive reactions. Others are complex behavior patterns—orientation to an adult's face or voice, or habituation to repeated stimulation. Still other observations have to do with how the baby organizes herself, how long she can stay alert, or how she attempts to console herself when she is upset. The examiner is also asked to be aware of which forms of adult behavior the newborn is most responsive to. All these observations help the examiner evaluate the baby's motor, cognitive, social, and temperamental individuality.

"The Brazelton" examiner rates each infant's performance on a set of twenty-seven behavioral scales. This provides grist for the research mill, a quantifiable method of comparing babies with one another. He also develops a general impression of the baby and how he might affect his environment through his unique way of expressing himself. These impressions are summarized in descriptive paragraphs highlighting the striking qualities of each baby's behavior.

To give you a taste of the flavor of these differences, here are evaluations of two newborn infants, both of whom were healthy and full-term.

This thin, wiry boy . . . was stringy and long in appearance, had a tense look and tense musculature. . . . His arms and legs seemed constantly in motion when he was awake. He had been in deep sleep when he was first approached but he awakened screaming. Periods of crying and sleeping alternated rapidly, and there was little opportunity to reach him during transitions from one to the other. In order to quiet him we had to swaddle him or hold him tightly or provide him with a pacifier and rock him. He startled and began to cry when disturbed by a rattle, voice, or sudden movement. He made little effort to quiet himself. This overreaction seemed to interfere with his ability to attend to auditory and visual stimuli, for when he was successfully restrained he could look around and attend to a face or a red ball, or turn toward the sound of a voice or a rattle. As soon as we realized this, his performance changed from an overreactive, hyperactive one to that of an alert, responsive baby.

This was a well-proportioned, active, responsive boy with an alert, inquisitive face, big dark eyes, and a shock of black hair. . . . As we played with him, he became more alert and on several occasions seemed to smile. . . . He maintained long periods of alertness. His main feature was his command of motor responsiveness. . . . After a startle and cry, he turned his head to one side and brought his hand up to his mouth to quiet himself. Even as he responded to visual and auditory stimulation with rapid attention and continuous responses, one felt that he had himself under control. A parent might feel that this was a mature, exciting boy, but she might also feel that he could manage pretty well by himself.

"The Brazelton" has had a tremendous impact on infant research. It has been a most powerful tool in two respects. First, it has "turned on" hundreds of scientists to the *marvelous* newborn. Few adults can spend a half hour playing intensely with a baby, as "the Brazelton" requires, and not come away acutely appreciative of the complexities of the newborn. Second, "the Brazelton" has contributed to a growing understanding about how the newborn's past may influence his ability to adapt to his new environment. Using "the Brazelton" with different groups of babies lets us compare these groups, and thus increase our ability to evaluate how various prenatal events—maternal alcoholism, malnutrition, or use of pain-relieving drugs—might influence baby behavior.

In a third respect, however, "the Brazelton" has not succeeded. As we have gained a fuller appreciation of all a newborn baby is capable of doing, we have also had to confront a tremendously important issue: how does a baby's initial personal style relate to his later style? In other words, can we examine a newborn today and make an accurate prediction about his future? The answer is essentially no. While a baby usually performs in a similar manner during separate tests in his first days of life, there can be striking differences, too. Sometimes we think we can justify the differences by pointing to an identifiable interfering event. For example, we might note that one day a baby was tested just after he was fed, and the next, just prior to a much-desired nursing; this might be an explanation for the baby's sucking on his own fist more during the second Brazelton assessment. More often, however, we cannot come up with a ready excuse. The baby himself—not just his environment—seems to be responsible for many of the variations in performance we observe.

The problems mount considerably when we dare to predict babies' personal styles over the weeks and months following their births. This is particularly difficult using standardized assessments like "the Brazelton," since babies rapidly outgrow the exam. By just one month of age, they have developed so many new behavior patterns and ways of organizing their activity that "the Brazelton" is no longer an adequate way of describing their capabilities. There are other means of assessing older infants, but these often tap different processes. Our ability to predict is hampered both by changes in the baby and changes in our assessment techniques.

Should Brazelton and his associates consider their efforts a failure? Is the lack of significant continuity in development revealed by our tests a sign of our inability to notice the critical aspects of early development? Here again we think the answer is no. Babies are, as Brazelton noted when he began to formulate his assessment technique, dynamic people. Using their marvelous response capacities, they can reorganize and develop rapidly in a new, very demanding environment. They accomplish this feat with our aid, by interacting with care-givers who each have an individual style. Thus, one of the major strengths of newborns is their ability to change so that they remain in tune with the people around them. If we tried to minimize this strength during our examination in order to create a sense of artificial continuity, our exam would be all the weaker.

The challenge for researchers is to draw a picture of the

newborn *changing*. We must learn to talk about developing individuals, not prematurely finished products. We must have the courage to look at each infant's future as open—a future that is in some respects hinted at by the baby's initial style in relating to a new world, but also a future that can never be confidently predicted.

Parents who have had the intimate experience of observing a newborn develop into a closely predicted child might wonder whether there still might not be a way to discuss the continuity of personality that they are certain they had perceived. Isn't there any way to get at the complex shaping of personality by the constant interplay of the baby's personal style and the specific people and events to which he or she is exposed?

This challenge has not gone unanswered by researchers. Perhaps the earliest method of describing the continuity of personality over all the changes of early childhood involved detailed diaries not so very different from the ones many parents keep. Using this case study procedure, it is difficult to compare one baby's developmental course with another. Yet its wealth of detail makes up for its poverty as an incisive research tool. A case study allows the researcher to focus on events that seem central to each particular baby so that a consistent, convincing portrait can be sketched. This flexibility has been particularly revealing when used to study a baby who is confronted with either unusual developmental obstacles, like blindness, or an atypical environment, such as care-giving by two blind parents.

Few researchers, however, are satisfied solely by the case-study method. They want to compare one infant with another to probe general principles concerning the development of individuality. As soon as they take this leap, however, they must confront problems much like those plaguing the use of "the Brazelton" in predicting a baby's future. Some decide to follow only a particular thread, such as a baby's activity level in response to the removal of a blanket, and then see how this relates to another response to a specific event months or years later. Sometimes relationships are found, but they may be rather weak and often very complex. Sometimes, moreover, the most striking finding is the reversal of the earlier relationship. The most active babies may turn out to be the least active two-year-olds—and then the most active four-year-olds.

Data from such studies are indeed puzzling. If you discover no (or very weak or very twisted) connections between specific early and later behavior patterns, does this mean that there are no real connections? Does it mean that there are many possible connections, depending on an unknown blending of the child's behavior and environmental events? If so, why do some case studies—as well as many parental reports and diaries—give so convincing a picture of continuity?

One common answer is that, while specific behavior patterns are transformed during development, underlying (or higher-order) qualities may still remain fairly consistent. This makes intuitive sense since, of course, babies do change their outward behavior patterns. They do, for example, rapidly develop new ways of moving about, their early total dependence on others gradually diminishing as they master turning over, crawling, and finally walking and running. Perhaps there is still some stable individual difference in how eager or how proficient a baby is in deploying these locomotive behavior patterns. Why not, then, trace qualities instead of specific actions?

This sort of logic has been used in the design of many large-scale projects that have attempted to trace the origins of personality. While none of these massive efforts has led to a grand solution for tracing continuity during development, many have made significant contributions to how we conceptualize the origins of temperamental qualities. They have provided us with the words to describe infants at different ages in such a way that we do not have to use a new vocabulary each time a baby develops a new skill.

The approach we find particularly appealing was formalized by Stella Chess, Alexander Thomas, and Herbert Birch of New York University Medical Center as they directed a study of the development of 141 children beginning when the children were two months old and ending when they were over ten years of age. The parents of each child consented to be interviewed repeatedly from the start. During each interview, they were asked specific questions about their baby's qualities. After each interview, researchers rated the baby high, medium, or low on nine characteristics that, for them, described the child's temperamental or behavioral profile.

Here are the nine temperament scales with examples of how two-month-olds might be rated.

Activity level. How much does your baby move throughout the day? A very active two-month-old might wiggle during sleep and during all care-giving activities, while an inactive peer might lie still.

Rhythmicity. How regular are your baby's cycles of sleep and wakefulness, excretion, hunger? Some infants' cycles are regular from the start, while other infants wake up at all hours and never seem to take the same amount of milk during their erratically spaced feedings.

Approach/Withdrawal. How does your baby respond to new objects and people? Some young infants greet any new event with glee, while others express distress, crying to each new person or spitting out any unfamiliar food.

Adaptability. With how much ease does your baby adapt to events? For example, after first objecting to a bath, some babies gradually get used to it and actually enjoy it by the age of two months, while others persistently find it cause for alarm.

Threshold of Responsiveness. How intense does a stimulus have to be to provoke a reaction? For example, does your two-month-old startle to every slight noise or do you have to yell to distract her?

Intensity of Reaction. Once your baby reacts, does he do so with energy? Some infants cry vigorously when displeased; others merely whimper softly.

Quality of Mood. How often is your baby friendly, pleasant, and joyful? How often is she irritable, unpleasant, and unfriendly? For example, does she smile and gurgle after a feed, or does she persist with her prenursing blues?

Distractibility. How much will an irrelevant event alter her behavior? For example, does your baby keep on nursing if you shift positions, or does she suddenly stop?

Attention Span and Persistence. How much time does your baby devote to an activity despite possible disruptions? One two-month-old might continue to look around the room for almost an hour while a second may seem to need constant entertainment and variety to remain so alert and calm.

One of the most intriguing aspects of Chess, Thomas, and Birch's vocabulary is that it seems to work for children of many ages. Of course, you need to look for different clues in children of different ages. When, for example, you try to decide how adaptable a child is, what you look for will depend very much on whether your subject is three months or three years old. But you can, nevertheless, usually decide how to describe your child's characteristics at any point in the developmental cycle, even when the baby is still very young. When Chess, Thomas, and Birch interviewed parents of two-month-old infants, they noticed that these adults had little problem informing them about their infants' typical reactions and habits. This does not mean that the babies' perceptual and motor abilities had not changed remarkably in the two months since birth, but rather that the babies each had nevertheless impressed close observers with the consistency of their temperaments.

Sometimes, of course, the baby's temperament was consistently inconsistent—that is, the infant was not establishing regular patterns. She might, for instance, have constantly kept her parents guessing about when a feeding would be requested or about which soothing technique might best help her fall asleep.

Chess, Thomas, and Birch's explanation of the development of temperament is similar to Brazelton's. They, too, argue that infants' initial behavior patterns engage and influence care-givers who in turn influence the baby's development. As parents with several children always notice, different children influence the same parent differently. A cuddly baby may be responded to with hugs, whereas a baby who fails to melt into your arms may cause you to find other ways, such as stroking or talking, to interact. But parents themselves come in more cuddly or less cuddly versions, and their preferred methods of interacting influence their babies' behavior. The baby's personality is not solely determined either by his original personal style or by those of his caregivers, but by a complicated and ever-changing blending of the two. A harmonious blend may be easier to achieve if, for example, a baby who startles to every noise is complemented by a quiet, methodical sort of parent, or if a baby with irregular behavior patterns is paired with parents who can tolerate some disorder in their routines. Mismatches, however, need not be disasters—and fortunately so, since they are so frequent. Parents can and do adapt to infants who are quite different from their "dream" baby—and their babies adapt to them. Since parents are the opportunity for the baby to form his own expressive style, he is inevitably influenced by their style. The same infant's temperament might even develop quite differently if we could somehow observe him in two different households.

The assessment methods of Brazelton, Chess, Thomas, and Birch have helped to develop a special attitude toward newborn individuality. While we should not deny that babies at birth are already unique individuals, we must not err in the other direction, concluding that their temperaments will not change over the years of their development. This attitude, intellectually most demanding, was captured by Richard Bell, a research psychologist, when he compared reading newborn behavior with reading a book. He noted that newborn behavior is more like a preface to a book than a table of its contents yet to be unfolded. "The preface is merely a rough draft undergoing rapid revision. [It contains] some clues to the nature of the book . . . but . . . taking them as literally prophetic is likely to lead to disappointment."

Parents may object to this cautious attitude since, unlike the researcher, they may feel they cannot afford to wait patiently to see how the entire story develops. Their very closeness to each infant demands that they try to make predictions about this individual even when the clues are vague

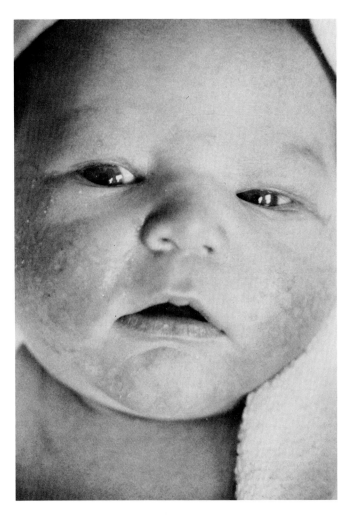

LEFT:
The newborn, with her puffed cheeks and red mottled skin, could hardly be described as beautiful, except by her parents.

BELOW LEFT:
Tongue protrusion in an alert newborn. It is claimed that infants are able to imitate the tongue protrusion of adults.

BELOW RIGHT:
A full cry, recognizable by sight and sound. An irresistible signal to parents.

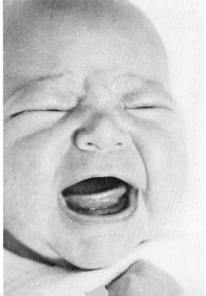

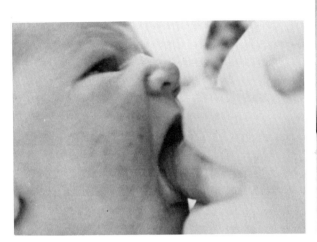

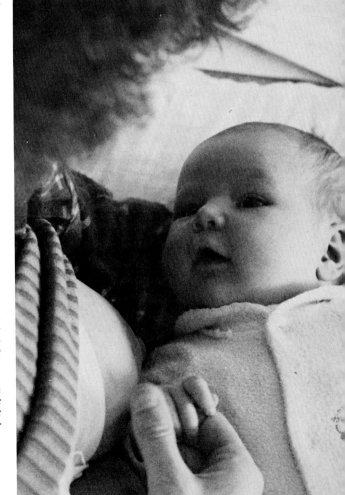

ABOVE:
The newborn opens her mouth wide, takes the nipple, makes a seal, and begins to suck in bursts.

RIGHT:
This is a very complex sequence of behavior that is often interrupted for social interaction.

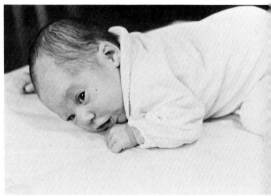

ABOVE AND RIGHT:
An infant changing from a sleep state to a fully awake state. As she grows more alert, muscle tone increases, she lifts her head, and her eyes widen to explore the world.

LEFT AND BELOW:
These photographs depict a sequence during which an infant frees her face after being placed in a prone position. Notice how she ends up sucking on her hand, a self-consoling maneuver to calm her distress.

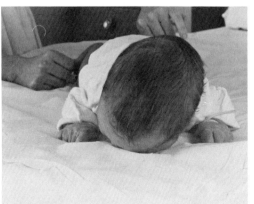

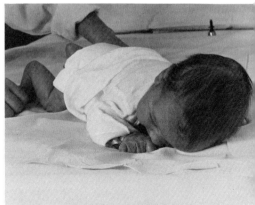

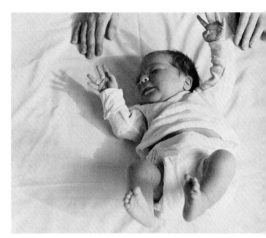

Infants are able to "walk," first lifting one leg then the other, when given the appropriate social and physical support.

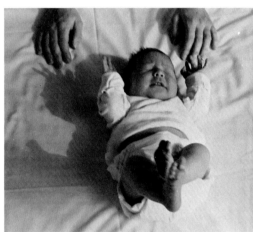

The infant reacts with a startle, or Moro, to the observer's slapping of the bed next to her ears. Her arms and legs flail outward and then come back to the midline.

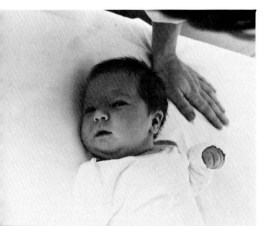

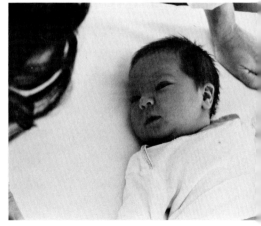

A newborn infant is able to follow a face with coordinated head-eye movements. Notice how the infant's eyebrows are raised, creating an intent, alert look.

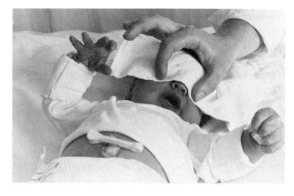

When a cloth is placed over an infant's face, the infant gets upset and makes swipes directed toward the cloth. Some infants succeed in batting it away. This reaction also occurs when the cloth does not cover the infant's nose or mouth and even when the cloth merely blocks the infant's vision.

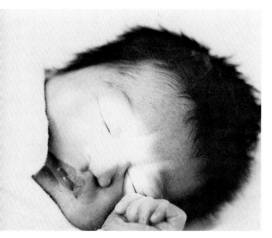

LEFT AND BELOW:
These photographs at left and below show three differents parts of the Brazelton examination. First, a bright light is flashed into an infant's closed eyes, causing him to screw up his face. After several repetitions, however, the infant will no longer react to the stimulus. In the two other pictures, the infant listens to a bell and looks at a bright red ball. The ability to shut out disturbing stimuli, such as the light, allows the infant to selectively react to more interesting stimuli, such as the bell and ball.

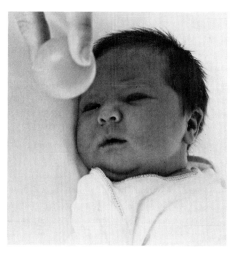

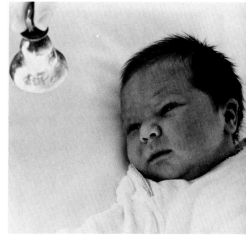

Four different infant reflexes, all part of a neurological exam and a Brazelton examination.

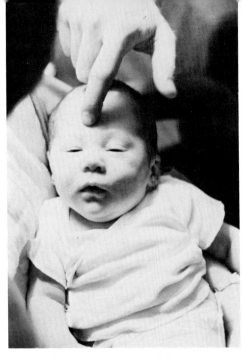

The glabella reflex is a closing of the eyes when the infant is lightly tapped on the forehead.

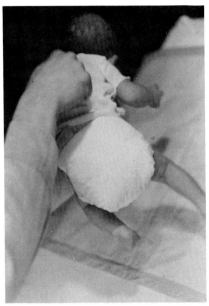

The incurvation reflex occurs when you firmly stroke the infant's back, producing a sharp hip swing toward the side stroked.

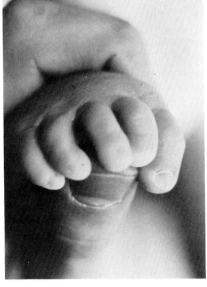

The planter grasp is produced when a finger is pressed on the sole of the infant's foot, and the palmar grasp results when a finger is pressed across the infant's palm. Notice how white the tips of the infant's toes and fingers are, indicating how strongly the infant is grasping.

Fathers bring something unique to their infants. They are more apt to jazz up the baby with poking, playful games.

Mothers carefully tailor their movements to suit the baby by slowing them down and exaggerating them. Here a mother imitates her baby's facial expression, smiles in response to his smile, and makes an "O" face at the peak of excitement in their interaction.

Babies are able to make wonderful faces, especially during social exchanges. ABOVE *we see amazement at what the partner is doing, and* BELOW *joy in being able to share in it.*

and insufficient. Even if they agree with Bell's attitude toward reading newborn behavior, they may still wish to pin special meaning on some of their newborn baby's attributes—if only for the sake of describing their new wonder to friends and relatives. They often solve this dilemma by concentrating on their baby's physical appearance.

Adults, of course, do not take seriously many of their newborn's vital statistics, although they may delight in discussing them. Few would put too much store on the future implications of their newborn's weight and indeed should not, no matter how much they might relish this magic number. Nevertheless, there are certain physical attributes which remain permanent and which we can easily define. Gender heads this list of promising clues.

Gender definitely has significant implications for the roles we play in our society throughout our life cycles. Yet, especially today, sex-related social roles are changing so rapidly that few adults would hope to predict how their newborns will be influenced by such social norms. There is, however, considerable controversy storming around the related issue of how psychological attributes are related to gender. While men and women certainly do not conform to stereotyped views of femininity and masculinity, no one yet understands how individual variations in aggressiveness and nurturance are gender-related.

Researchers studying newborn infants are in a unique position to explore this issue. Using Bell's analogy, they can try to see how gender initially relates to individual newborn behavior. They can watch how care-givers use the gender code as they describe and interact with their newborns. And then they can try to discern any systematic relationship between the care-givers' perceptions of the code and how individual infants develop.

If there are really clear-cut sex differences apparent in the way newborns behave, we would be in a privileged position to follow the development of any psychological individual difference that is tied to a clear-cut physical sign. What a simple way to trace babies developmentally! But no such easy way out is possible. It turns out that if we are unaware of a baby's sex, we cannot tell by observing the infant's behavior if he or she is a boy or a girl. In study after study, we have found very few reliable sex differences. Even when we use such a sensitive assessment technique as "the Brazelton," we are at a loss to distinguish girls from boys without taking a look at physical signs. Those few differences that are found tend to be both very fragile (difficult to find again unless you do exactly the same thing that the first researcher did) and very subtle (evident only when we look at many infants, since the overlap of what boys and girls do is very marked).

Some researchers argue that, despite the sparse evidence concerning newborn sex differences, a pattern of findings gradually emerges when many studies are reviewed. Anneliese Korner of Stanford University, for example, thinks that we have enough evidence to conclude that boy babies have greater muscular strength and that girls are more responsive to touch and to oral stimulation—clues she feels might link up with reports of differences between older girls and boys. She admits that her evidence is so far quite weak. For example, her claim about girls' greater tendency to respond to oral stimulation comes from research reporting that girl newborns tend to make more reflexive smiles when they sleep, that they more often suck rhythmically, and that they often evidence a greater preference for sweet drinks. The conclusion that boys are stronger is based on research demonstrating that boys more often hold their heads up high when they are placed on their stomachs. Korner finds these clues sufficiently intriguing, however. She believes the known hormonal differences in the prenatal environments of boys and girls could be responsible for these behavioral differences.

Korner's general perspective can (and has been) heatedly disputed. Yet, even some strong opponents have admitted that she may be correct in suggesting that there are subtle differences in the central nervous system's organization in male and female newborns. A number of physical traits support this basic claim. For example, girl newborns are, on the average, more physically mature (as indicated by bone development) than boys, a variance that persists throughout most of childhood. Male infants more often need special medical assistance during the newborn period. They are, as a group, more vulnerable to various genetic disorders, and they seem more sensitive to various physiological stresses that may occur before or during birth. Yet, once again, we are unable to extrapolate confidently from the body of research now available to any reliable statements about sex-related psychological or behavioral differences.

While the studies on newborn sex-related behavioral differences are baffling and controversial, the research findings on how adults perceive these elusive "differences" is not. We adults do not treat the sex of a baby as a trivial clue. To us, it is a central organizer, a potent description of who the newborn baby is.

Just how much we read into an infant's gender has been demonstrated beautifully by a simple study performed in Boston by Jeffry Rubin, Frank Provenzano, and Zella Luria. They began with the notion that babies at birth are so "undifferentiated" that we could barely tell them apart if we were not so very motivated to do so. Adults nevertheless search for distinctive features, and they find a convenient one in infants' genders. Once they know the sex of a baby (and they inevitably ask immediately), they then take "nature's first projective test." They invest the clue "girl" or "boy" with surplus meaning by making a host of assumptions based on current sex-role stereotypes.

To document this claim, Rubin and his coworkers interviewed thirty pairs of parents on the day of their first baby's birth. The male and female infants in this study did not differ from each other in body length, weight, or basic health. Yet, you would never know this from the ways the parents rated their babies on a questionnaire consisting of eighteen pairs of opposite words, such as "strong-weak," "big-little," and "hardy-delicate." While all the proud parents did apparently find their offspring to be "delightful, competent new additions to the world," their appraisals of their infants were colored by their knowledge of their babies' sex. Daughters were, in contrast to sons, considered "softer, finer-featured, littler, and more inattentive." Fathers, who had not yet had their wives' opportunities to interact with the babies, were most prone to such stereotyping. Further, a parent's own sex seemed to influence his or her view of the infant. One particularly amusing example of this was dubbed the "Oedipal effect": mothers rated sons as cuddlier than daughters while fathers rated daughters as cuddlier than sons!

Yet, according to most researchers, we cannot accurately distinguish girl from boy newborns by observing behavior alone. They may behave somewhat differently, but these differences are so subtle that we could argue endlessly about how to define them. On the other hand, care-givers seem to consider gender to be a most valuable clue to individual differences. At least when a researcher hands them a questionnaire, they make judgments that are influenced significantly by their knowledge of which half of humanity their infants belong to.

What happens, then, when such unisex-behaving newborns actually interact with their sex-stereotyping care-givers? Do the care-givers act according to their stated attitudes, or are their actions divorced from their opinions? And can very minute sex-related differences in newborn behavior provide the starting point for developmental interactions that support care-giver expectations?

It takes great courage to attack the research that addresses these questions. Since baby sex is such a certain variable, almost every study on care-giver and newborn interaction pays it at least cursory attention. We are burdened with literally hundreds of reports that might be relevant to our issue. And, unfortunately, these reports provide us with a most inconsistent picture, due, more often than not, to the researchers' use of different measures on different populations of babies and parents.

Eleanor Maccoby and Carol Jacklin of Stanford University braved this sea of data in hopes of coming up with an adequate summary. Considering studies that spanned all of childhood, they made table after table, charting studies that found significant behavioral differences based on sex against those that didn't. Unexpected as it may seem, they concluded that parent behavior was seldom affected by their infant's sex. In other words, despite parents' stated sex-typed anticipations and convictions, they usually do not treat girls differently from boys.

Two general trends have, however, been noted in a few major projects: mothers tend to touch their male newborns more than their female newborns; and they tend to talk and smile more to newborn girls than to newborn boys.

Why might mothers hold male infants more than female infants? It is hard to explain this finding in terms of our prevalent sex-role stereotypes. Maybe Korner provides an explanation: if boys are less sensitive to tactile stimulation than girls, stimulating a boy to an equivalent degree would require more touching and holding. Robert Emde offers another explanation: maybe the tendency for girls to be more mature at birth translates into behavioral differences that, while subtle, still inform the attentive mother that their girls are more able to attend to such sensory stimulation as talking, and less in need of physically supportive touching to remain organized and alert.

Notice that both explanations look at how very subtle differences in newborn behavior influence a mother's caregiving techniques. To research the question, we therefore need to trace the dynamics of the care-giver–baby interaction. This project is consistent with the theoretical insights of Brazelton, and Chess, Thomas, and Birch.

Such a project is also a practical nightmare. Babies differ from one another at any one age, and develop so rapidly that they change behavior every few weeks. Parents, too, are undeniably different from one another. And, since they are responsive people, they treat babies of different ages differently. Put together these sources of variation and it is extremely difficult to document the role an infant's sex might play.

Howard Moss of the National Institute of Mental Health nevertheless set out to document the development of this complex socialization network. He realized that to do so he would have to look in several directions simultaneously. He would have to figure out baby changes over weeks or months, and at the same time he could not ignore parent changes during that period. Most importantly, he did not want to dismiss mutual influences: how infants socialize their mothers while the mothers are socializing them.

Moss gathered an enormous body of data. Part of it consisted of detailed records of how thirty first-time mothers and their three-week-old babies spent a "typical" eight hours together. He returned for another eight-hour observation when the infants were three months old. The results are so rich that a simple summary hardly does them justice. But, if one point about sex differences stands out, it is that male and female infants do behave differently very early on, and that these differences influence how mothers react to their babies.

At three weeks of age, male babies tended to be fussier and more difficult to calm than were female babies. Girls tended to sleep about an hour longer during the eight hours of observation. These differences in behavior were apparent even though there was astonishing variability for each behavior observed. For example, one wonderful three-week-old fussed and cried only 5 minutes, while a peer was irritable for 136 minutes! Not surprisingly, babies had changed considerably by their observation at three months. Now they were crying less, awake more, and sending mothers more grins and gurgles. Once again, however, boys distinguished themselves from girls by being, on the average, more irritable and less sleepy.

Mothers were responsive to these differences, particularly when their infants were only three weeks old. At that time, male infants were held more, attended to more, stimulated and moved more. Moss performed complicated statistical feats to discern how baby moods and mother moods might be related. Mothers did appear to react responsively to infant moods at three weeks. For example, when three-week-old babies cried, they received maternal contact, and, since boys cried more than girls, they received more attention.

But the mothers, it turned out, were not completely under the control of their babies. Moss unraveled yet another striking relationship: when girls were three weeks old, as well as when they were three months old, he could predict how much handling they would receive from their mothers by looking at how irritable they were. This was not, however, true for the male infants: the mothers responded to their cries at three weeks but, at three months, the more often a boy cried the *less* his mother attended to him and handled him. Moss thought that perhaps girl babies were more likely to quiet down when their mothers tried to console them, and so, of course, mothers felt great satisfaction consoling them when they cried. But boys were less "reinforcing." A mother's cuddle might not so readily lead to quieting. After three months of such lessons, the mothers perhaps decided that they might just as well not respond. A cycle of inter-action—different for boys and girls—gradually emerged from these rather minor initial differences between the sexes.

Exciting as this project was, Moss was not willing to shut the case on the influence of sex differences on care-giving behavior. He led several additional investigations to refine his view. Each contributed new snags and threw a bit more light on the complex array of variables involved in the develop-ment of an individual child. After several years, he concluded that sex-related differences are initially moderate, at most. They can diminish or even disappear if the context changes. Or, they can be heightened, especially in situations that put stress on babies and thus feed into the male infants' relatively greater physiological vulnerability.

Despite so many attempts to unravel the influence of gender on a baby's developing personality, we are far from a full understanding of the processes involved. For anyone who seeks a simple explanation, even studies as revealing as Moss's must seem disappointing. This sorry state of affairs is perhaps even more pronounced when other areas of individuality, such as variations in intellectual development, are researched. Here we are stymied from the start, since babies do not pro-vide us with clear physical clues about the initial status of these elusive qualities. Much work remains to be done merely to define the very phenomena we wish to explore.

Even though we can draw only premature conclusions about how each baby develops his or her unique personality, we do believe that considerable progress has been made by recent research. A new perspective seems to be emerging as researchers become more willing to view babies as human beings who develop in human contexts. They seem more open to viewing each infant as a richly unique individual. And they are now more concerned with how individual caregivers influence and are influenced by individual babies. Finally, we see a new concern, among researchers, with the influence of culture on how adults interpret the significance of their babies' gender and behavior patterns.

Paradoxically, this new perspective promises to make life even more difficult for researchers. As it redirects our efforts, we can no longer be comfortable studying babies isolated from other humans, even when what we want to investigate is individuality. Nor will we be satisfied with explaining personality development as something babies accomplish on their own or as something we do for or to our babies. Rather, we can now see how each infant brings his or her own uniqueness to a unique social setting that simultaneously supports, changes, and fosters the infant's development. This may be a difficult perspective, but it contains the important ingredient of individuality.

6. Some Call It Sleep

Naive adults often believe that baby humans spend their first days sleeping. They know that certain unavoidable disturbances, such as an empty stomach, will disrupt the monotony of the infant's existence. Yet, they cling to the romantic view that if a care-giver shields the newborn from the challenges of the world, the baby will spend most of his time enjoying tensionless, blissful slumber.

Parents-to-be have ample evidence to discredit this image. Beginning with the first astonishing stirs of quickening, the pregnant woman can sense the actions of her child. And, as the squirms increase in intensity and as the small, sudden jerks gradually become pronounced and sustained kicks, others can share in observing the fetal dance.

Most expectant parents monitor their unborn child's movements carefully, even responding to a kick by pushing back against a fetal foot or knee. The fetus may seem to be quite responsive, obligingly shifting position when touched through his mother's abdominal wall, reacting to a loud noise, or even hiccuping after his mother indulges in a particularly exotic meal. The infant's strength as he adds full flips and distinct jabs to his repertoire is often reassuring, while long periods of apparent inactivity may be worrisome.

Some experienced parents contend that fetal movements provide clues about the baby's future style. Will he or she be athletic or lackadaisical, a go-getter or a happy-go-lucky type? Some parents are so certain of the validity of their first impressions that they will claim it's possible to learn about a child's adolescence by assessing activities in the womb.

Pleasurable as the jouncing and the speculations may be, the fetus may occasionally be rather bothersome, for while he often settles down when the mother is alert and active, he may spend his evenings literally jumping around. Though this may be a hint that he is already developing cycles of activity and quiescence, he does not yet impress us with his ability to synchronize with our adult patterns of daytime action and nighttime rest. New parents rarely find it possible, however, to check their fond speculations about their baby's style. Once born, the baby follows a most unadultlike pattern of sleep and wakefulness that interferes with thoughtful monitoring. For the weeks subsequent to birth, few problems will occupy parents more than the difference between their baby's cycle of waking and sleeping, and their own diurnal pattern.

Researchers have tended to be suspicious of parental interpretations of fetal activity. They have not, until recently, attempted to bridge the gap between the fetus's cycle of activity and the newborn's during each twenty-four-hour period. Yet, in their ever-cautious manner, researchers are—without going so far as predicting who will become football players and ballerinas—now beginning to make out the connections between fetal activity and the activity of the very young infant. What they are observing in their controlled monitoring of many babies, before and after birth, supports the essence of parents' claims after their own intimate exposure to the individual child—that there is indeed a link between the fetus's activity inside the womb and the baby's activity outside. This research highlights the remarkable organizational capacities of the fetus and the newborn. It promises, in fact, to reshape our view of the important links between life before and after birth and between infants and their care-givers.

During your baby's first weeks outside the womb, you make hundreds of appropriate judgments about what your baby is doing. It is usually easy to determine if he is asleep, awake, or crying—so easy in fact that it may hardly seem worth mentioning. Yet, as you make such obvious assessments, you are assuming that he is organizing his actions into repeatable patterns of behavior. By doing so, a baby takes it upon himself to help modulate his availability to outside events. Sleeping and crying are, in part, ways of shutting out disturbances and of defending his fragile organization from insult. Alertness is a way of beckoning to the world, of openly greeting it. When alert, he is better able to move smoothly, follow objects with his eyes, accurately locate sounds, and sustain social interactions.

The baby's remarkable ability to "self-organize" long escaped the notice of most researchers. Unlike parents, however, extreme familiarity was not to blame. Rather, their theoretical assumptions about the baby's inherent disorganization masked the signs that babies were, to a considerable degree, capable of internal control over their arousal level. When such theoretically blinded researchers looked to explain why it was often possible to predict what a baby would do during the coming few hours, they tended to watch what adults did rather than to credit the infant. When they were interested in organized action patterns, they were more likely to zero in on the movement of the baby's foot than to take an expansive look at the sequencing of the infant's moods. Impressed with the baby's seeming lack of stable terrain, they did not pay heed to the larger landscape of baby behavior.

By the mid-1960s, researchers took pride in noticing what previous colleagues had ignored. Evidence had been accumulating that even the smallest, most discrete behavior pattern, such as toe spreading in the Babinski reflex, could only be fully understood if studied within the context of the baby's overall actions. Two words were added to every baby-watcher's vocabulary: rhythm and state.

"Rhythm"—the cyclical repetition of certain behavior patterns—is evident in just about all baby activity. In fact, baby behavior appears to be organized into several simul taneous rhythms. Their actions possess a flow, which often makes it possible to predict what they just did and what they will do based on what they are now doing; even while they are alert, we know that they probably will next fuss, and then cry, and, finally, sleep. The rhythm of components within an action may be rapid. Thus, babies suck in regularly spaced but fairly rapid bursts and pauses, and they cry in pulses of repeated refrains. We can detect even finer-grained cycles (called microrhythms by some) when we monitor physiological processes, such as heartbeats or brain waves. Or, the perspective can be broadened to explore rhythms that take many minutes or even hours to complete their cycle; these macrorhythms gradually approach what parents so avidly seek—the diurnal cycle of our adult existence.

At any one time, the researcher can conceptually stop the constant flow of behavior and analyze many rhythms. The rhythms form in babies, as they do in us, a hierarchy: the fastest, smallest rhythms, such as heartbeats, are subsumed within the more prolonged ones, such as sleeping and waking. But, for the new baby, the project of forming a hierarchy of rhythms carries with it special demands. First, he must rapidly resynchronize his rhythms after birth. For example, in the uterus the fetus sucks, and makes respiratory efforts, though his lungs are not yet expanded to take in air. But only at birth must the newborn coordinate these two efforts and put them to work. (If he fails to, he will be constantly plagued by unpleasant occurences such as gulping of air instead of milk.) In addition to coordinating his own actions, he must quickly adopt his initial newborn rhythmic patterns so that they conform, at least approximately, to the pulse of the rest of the world.

"State" is a term that describes behavior clustered into a number of relatively discrete, relatively stable constellations. The names commonly used for the various states of newborns reveal just how commonsensical the researcher's recent perception of baby behavior is. For example, the time the newborn spends awake is often subdivided into four states: drowsy (eyelids drooping, muscles relaxed); alert (wide-eyed and still); fussy (squirming and complaining); and crying. We could provide you with more detailed criteria for identifying each of these states, but we bet you scarcely need them!

The baby's sleeping periods can also be divided into states. Typically, two are identified. "Quiet sleep" is the portion of your baby's day that you may come to appreciate with considerable relief. During quiet sleep her breathing is regular and she makes few spontaneous movements except for an occasional jerky startle. She appears to be "sleeping like a baby," an angel oblivious to all the earthly disturbances around her. The other sleep state has been called many names, including "light," "active," or "irregular" sleep. The name that covers this sleeping state's most intriguing feature is "REM [for Rapid Eye Movement] sleep." During REM sleep, a baby's eyes dart around under her closed eyelids. When adults make such rapid eye movements, they often, if awakened, report that they have been dreaming. We can only wonder if babies experience the same sensations during REM sleep, and, if so, what their first dreams are like.

It is tempting to arrange states on a continuum of activity with quiet sleep at one end and crying at the other. This may not, however, be accurate. Even quiet sleep is not a state of stillness or static existence, since it takes effort not to be disturbed by outside noises or even by the discomfort of lying in one position for a long time, and to keep such internal activities as digestion and elimination under control. There is, moreover, a paradox regarding the baby's sleep states which only becomes apparent when you hook the baby up to a special monitor for recording brain waves and muscle tone. Since the brain does some of its work with electrical energy, the brain's pattern of electrical energy can be graphed by a procedure known as an electroencephalogram—EEG for short. When an EEG is made for a sleeping baby, we can see that, consistent with the continuum idea, the brain-wave pattern shows more activity during REM sleep than during quiet sleep. Indeed, the brain-wave patterns in REM sleep look very much like the brain-wave patterns of a baby in an alert state. However, if you also monitor the baby's muscle tone, you discover that REM sleep is the state during which the baby displays the least muscle tone. In one sense the baby seems most relaxed, and in another quite busy.

There is another puzzling relationship between baby state and baby behavior. Newborns do not always react in the same way to the same stimulus. For example, if you shake a rattle near an alert newborn's ear, he may become very still and then slowly orient his face toward the sound. The rattle's noise may soothe him when he is fussy. Yet, when the same baby is in a state of quiet sleep, he may not react at all, or he may merely startle once or twice. The relationship between state and reactivity is also not simple. For example, the knee-jerk reflex, which is crisp and strong when a baby is quietly asleep, and moderately intense when he is alert, proves surprisingly difficult to elicit during REM sleep. Other reflexes have different patterns. For example, rooting, hand-grasping, and the Babkin reflex (a curious response pattern where the baby leans his head forward and opens his mouth when his palms are pressed) can all be obtained most readily during the alert state, less easily during REM sleep, and with extreme difficulty during quiet sleep.

Despite such difficulties with the idea of a simple continuum, the concept of state is too valuable to discard. Using it, we can summarize many variations in baby behavior much more readily than if we did not take note of the baby's overall state when we try to elicit a particular reaction. It is nevertheless important to realize that there is no satisfactory explanation of the underlying mechanisms of state regulation. While the recognition that infant behavior patterns cluster rather neatly into states has been a major step toward describing how newborn activity is organized, it also makes us all the more aware of the baby's mysteries.

Combining the two concepts of "rhythm" and "state" raises one of the most fascinating questions about newborn infants: what are the rhythms of a baby's states? In other words, what is the temporal pattern of a baby's sleep-wake cycles, and how does it change during early infancy? Parents only mildly bothered by a lack of evening synchrony before their baby was born may wearily confront this issue as they try to synchronize their own schedules with those of the newborn. Researchers have begun to study just this process of synchrony, for the phenomenon of how babies become daytime people seems to be a relatively untapped goldmine of clues to how newborns regulate themselves to mesh with the rhythms of others.

To begin with, researchers have had to arm themselves with some basic facts. For example, how much of each day do babies devote to their various "states"? While this is a simple question, it requires considerable stamina to answer. Nathaniel Kleitman and his coworkers at the University of Chicago were among the first researchers to tackle it when, over thirty years ago, they observed babies around the clock. Although we now have some very elaborate, automatic ways of monitoring baby states, Kleitman's estimates are still reliable: newborns sleep about sixteen to seventeen hours out of every twenty-four. Over the first four months of life, this total decreases by about an hour, and after six months, the baby sleeps about fourteen hours out of every twenty-four, or about 60 percent of the time.

Researchers estimate that almost 50 percent of sleep time is spent in REM sleep if the infants are born at term. Premature babies devote even more sleep time to REM sleep. That newborns spend half their sleep time in REM sleep is quite intriguing, since by three months of age full-term babies will cut that percentage in half, and by adulthood only about 13 percent of their sleep time will be REM sleep. This represents a decline from almost eight hours per day-night cycle to under two hours. Despite these striking differences, however, it probably is not accurate to conclude that babies are lost in dreams. Many physiologists now speculate that this sleeping baby with a paradoxically active brain may be self-stimulating such critical brain development as the growth of connections between brain nerve cells.

After devoting some sixteen hours to sleep, the newborn infant has only about eight hours out of the twenty-four to divide among the four states of wakefulness. Crying and fussing claim the largest chunk of this time; babies often cry lustily for about an hour and a half every twenty-four hours during the first three months after birth. This figure escalates discouragingly to about two and a half hours of crying per twenty-four at six weeks, but it then mercifully declines to about an hour of wailing by four-month-olds. The least prevalent state in the newborn period is alertness. While we do know that its total duration increases steadily over the first weeks of life, the amount of time spent greeting the world alertly is quite dependent on what the care-giver does with the baby.

As we rattle off these statistics, you may be finding it difficult to recognize your own baby in them. For one thing, we are using average figures, and, as we have often noted, there is amazing variability among newborns. Some babies, especially if they are on a demand feeding schedule, may cry as little as a few minutes: others unfortunately may cry for hours. Some babies sleep over twenty hours out of every twenty-four, while others get along on only eleven hours' sleep. In addition, while an average of sixteen hours of sleep may sound like bliss, that sleep time may be chunked together or sprinkled over the entire day-night cycle—two very different things. Babies make no secret of opting for the latter pattern. During the newborn period, the average longest stretch of sleep rarely exceeds four hours. The trend toward longer stretches is hardly steady, but most infants do sleep up to six hours at a time by their eighth week, and by four months they may achieve a record of eight or even more hours. It also takes time to consolidate periods of brief wakefulness into longer wakeful stretches. Newborns remain awake for only short spans of at most two hours; they gradually increase their longest waking period to about three or four hours' duration by the time they start to sleep for eight.

These additional averages may still do little justice to your experience caring for a new baby. After all, what comfort is it to share a two-hour alert period between the hours of midnight and 2 A.M., or to watch your baby peacefully sleep away the entire morning? Certainly, the most impressive feature of a baby's rhythm of states is the synchronization (or its absence) of your two schedules.

Fitting your baby's sleep-wake rhythms to yours or yours to his occurs only gradually, through a process of mutual adaptation. While you may only become fully aware of the frustrations of this process once your baby is born, it actually has a long history. Researchers have evidence that, while still a fetus, your child is practicing some of the critical capacities which he will need to mobilize in order to become a daytime person. In the uterus the fetus is already actively modulating his reactions to outside stimulation. Such modulation after birth involves the baby's attending selectively to certain stimuli, or his adapting to a repeated stimulus by gradually diminishing the intensity of his reactions. This ability to get used to repeated stimulation is known as habituation, and it is an ability newborns readily display. For example, if you shine a flashlight briefly toward your sleeping baby's eyes, he may first acknowledge its presence with a squirm, eye-squinting, and other appropriate behavior. But as you repeat this outside insult, the baby may gradually stop reacting and act as though he does not notice. He may not respond by awakening, but neither has he indiscriminately shut out the whole world. You can observe this by shaking a rattle near his ear once he no longer reacts to the light. Most likely, he will once again react with full force and then gradually shut the rattle out as well. When your baby is awake, should any sight or sound, even an attractive one, persist for too long, he can stop reacting to it and still pay heed to any new sensation that comes his way.

Such abilities are essential if your baby is to organize her states into a pattern, for they allow her to have some internal control over her level of arousal when outside stimuli are potentially disruptive. Once you have observed your own baby habituate, you can have little doubt that very young babies, once born, are both selectively responsive and relatively well organized when they react.

It is much harder to get a fetus to demonstrate that he, too, is able to control what he takes notice of and to become accustomed to repeated stimulations. While babies before birth are not protected by a "placental barrier" (once thought automatically to shut them off from chemicals, noises, and so forth when in fact they are not even shut off from light, since the mother's stretched skin is translucent), their privileged position of safety within the womb does make it extremely difficult to transform them into research subjects. Nevertheless, there are now a number of ways we can monitor their activity in the uterus and, by combining the results of these methods, we can be fairly sure that unborn babies demonstrate the rudiments of the newborn's capabilities.

One of the first scientific reports of fetal responsivity confirmed what pregnant women often report. By altering their activity level, unborn babies sometimes respond to what mothers hear and ingest; they may even respond to her emotions in this way. Lester Sontag made careful recordings of fetal movements and heartbeat rate as he presented different types of stimulation. One of his most dramatic demonstrations of how babies respond to outside stimulation entailed presenting different sounds and vibration patterns to the fetus through the mother's abdominal wall. Even when a mother could not hear the sound, the baby responded with increased movement and an accelerated heartbeat rate. When the sound was audible to the mother, the baby still reacted too rapidly to have been influenced by the mother's own reactions.

Sontag was experimenting in the 1930s, so he was only able to get in touch with the fetus rather indirectly. Now we have more sophisticated methods, which allow us to spy on the fetus more intimately but without too much disturbance. One is called ultrasound, a technique that uses a high-frequency sound to take a picture of the fetus in much the same way scientists use sonar to map territory underwater. Using this technique, we see that the fetus startles when exposed to a bright light shining through the mother's translucent abdominal skin, a push against the uterus, or a sudden loud noise. In fact, medical examination of the fetus using ultrasound often begins by "waking the fetus up" with a bell. Ultrasound also reveals that the fetus can modulate her responsivity. If a soft light or sound is directed through the side of the mother's abdomen, the fetus may gradually turn smoothly toward it. This well-organized response is easier to elicit when the fetus is still than when she is squirming and kicking, a striking parallel to the different response of the newborn in alert and fussy states.

We would learn much about the prenatal "states" if we could invade the fetus's privacy even more and record how his brain waves are changing in relation to his movements. We have to wait until he is about to be born to do so, however. Then it is possible to attach sensors to his scalp as it is crowning. The situation is far from ideal, since labor and delivery undoubtedly put the baby under considerable stress. Nevertheless, electrical brain waves even during birth alter according to what the baby hears, and how he is touched.

One more approach to figuring out what the fetus responds to has been developed: babies' experiences before birth are studied in terms of their possible influence on their behavior after birth. As mentioned in chapter four, a particularly clever report of this method was published by two Japanese scientists, Y. Ando and H. Hattori. They wanted to find out if intense noise during fetal life affected how babies adapted to noise after birth. To do this, they studied two groups of infants. The first group had spent their prenatal months near the Osaka airport, while the second had lived in quieter surroundings. Babies from both groups were delivered at a hospital located under a flight pattern. Prenatal experience seemed to make a significant difference in how the two groups spent their first days after birth. Those infants who were used to plane noise were over five times more likely to sleep through the sound of a plane overhead. They woke up crying to only one out of every ten planes, while their inexperienced peers awoke screaming to almost 50 percent of the planes. This suggests to us that the fetus may be able to habituate much as he will after birth.

The research we have considered so far supports our claim that unborn babies have at least the most basic ability to process stimulation selectively and to modulate their responses—talents that will be essential when they first live in our busy world. Since, however, we have been observing them for only the brief periods during which we control the outside stimulation, our research does not tell us how fetuses routinely organize their behavior when researchers are not flashing lights and ringing bells. There are two ways to chart this routine.

First, the researcher can wait until the baby is born and, if birth occurs early, watch how these premature babies (of comparable age to most fetuses) organize their states. These premature infants presumably have the same abilities as the fetus. But interpreting what premature babies do in their new environment as indicative of what fetuses do in the womb is fraught with difficulties. For example, premature infants spend more time in REM sleep than do full-term infants. They are also more likely to spend time in states that we cannot readily classify using the categories established for older infants. Is the state regulation of premature babies really typical of babies of the same age still in the womb? To what extent might the premature babies be mobilizing regulatory mechanisms prematurely?

Second, the researcher can try to muster the patience to monitor fetal activity constantly over many hours. This is no simple task because, of course, we cannot perform our research without the most active involvement of the mother. W.B. Sterman and his colleagues at the University of California in Los Angeles did team up with eight extraordinarily cooperative women to amass some truly astonishing data. Three to five times during the last four months of their pregnancies these women slept, attached to an array of machines, in the university's sleep laboratory. Three electrodes were taped to their abdomens so that researchers could keep constant tabs on fetal movement. Other electrodes were simultaneously recording the mother's overall movements, her brain waves, eye movements, and other evidence of her activity level. A total of thirty nights of recording were collected and then analyzed in detail to see how the fetuses were patterning their movements.

A fetus may have his own beat, his mother hers. Yet, because of the close contact between the two, the fetal pattern may be influenced by the mother's, and thus changed from what it would be were he a totally autonomous person. The first task was to find the underlying rhythm of the fetal cycle as the fetus swung from the least active to the most active states. Then it was necessary to discern the rhythm of the mother's cycle as she, too, swung from least active to most active sleep, and finally to see in what ways the mother's rhythm might influence her unborn child's. Sterman found that even his youngest subjects, fetuses only twenty-one weeks old, were systematically clustering their periods of activity and rest throughout the night.

By employing a very complex method of charting the waves of activity and rest, Sterman was able to discern two different cycles. During the longer of the two cycles, it took the baby about one and a half hours to perform a full pattern from least to most active. The shorter cycle of rest and activity lasted about forty minutes. He also looked at how these two cycles related to the mother's cycle of least active quiet sleep to most active REM sleep and, sometimes, to a state of alertness. When the fetus, in his forty-minute cycle, reached a peak in activity that occurred simultaneously with his mother's most active phase of REM sleep, that peak was higher than it would otherwise have been. When his peak was reached at the same time his mother was entering a phase of deep slumber, his own activity level was somewhat suppressed. Thus, the fetus's short underlying rhythm was augmented by the mother's longer cycle, making his rest more restful if his mother was resting, his activity more zestful if his mother was in active REM sleep. This evidence clearly supports the impressions of many pregnant women who claim that while they are dreaming their unborn babies dance most furiously. Moreover, these findings indicate that, even before birth, babies are able to mesh their cycles with those of others, even though the babies do not sleep through the night as their mothers do.

The shorter cycle seems to be the fetus's very own, as it does not match the mother's cycle of rest and activity. In fact, the longer cycle disappears at birth when the baby is separated from the mother, while this forty-minute cycle persists. Sterman's fetal subjects were introduced at birth to Arnold

Parmalee and he then studied their continued cycles of activity and rest. The similarities between Sterman's short-cycle observations and Parmalee's data on newborn cycles were marked. Indeed, one subject even displayed identical cycle durations (to the minute) during his gestation and just after birth.

The longer, one-and-a-half-hour cycle of fetal activity and rest indicates that our adult cycles can influence—perhaps through chemical messages or even perceptual clues—unborn children. But the shorter, forty-minute cycle suggests that the control is by no means all ours. Rather, babies are born with an internal clock, their own fundamental cycle of rest and activity. The factors responsible for the presence of this built-in control remain a mystery. As Sterman cogently concluded, this cycle may prove to be the "biological missing link," the most basic pacemaker, that guides infants' self-regulation as they adapt to their postbirth environment.

After months of meshing his cycles with his mother's, the fetus receives a rude shock. Suddenly his most intimate connection with adult cycles is severed, and he must mobilize new mechanisms to again establish a pattern that conforms to both his own fundamental cycles and his care-givers' rhythms. For weeks after birth, no process will occupy babies and care-givers more fully than the negotiation of a new relationship between infant and adult cycles. Eating, sleeping, and playing all become involved, for each must be addressed within the overall temporal framework.

We usually think of babies' becoming daytime people in terms of milestone achievements. From this perspective, newborns look quite disorganized. For example, common wisdom from both inside and outside the laboratory predicts that infants will not come to respect twenty-four-hour diurnal cycles until they are about three months old, even when care-givers try hard to convince them to do so. In one sense, mothers may be prepared, by their own frequent nighttime waking and daytime napping late in pregnancy, for similarly unusual cycles after their babies are born. But adults certainly become stressed by the lack of synchrony between their cycles and the infants's; their infants' gradual adaptation to diurnal cycles may seem filled with frustrating regressions and inexplicable fluctuations.

Looking only at fluctuations, however, tends to blind us to the rapidity with which newborns begin to mesh cycles with us. They are actually remarkably successful in a very short time. Yet, since gathering adequate data proves discouragingly time consuming, we are only beginning to understand how the negotiation process proceeds.

Nevertheless, not all researchers have shied away from the challenge of studying the negotiation process in action. One in particular, Louis Sander, has devoted over a decade to just this issue. His work illustrates well the fruits of combining theory with research.

Sander began with one central idea: the newborn baby is not an isolated being, but one who exists in a living system with her care-givers. We shouldn't isolate her from others or break her behavior down into isolated variables. Moreover, time is critical to a living system, and "the temporal organization of events constitutes a domain of order that cannot be in any way neglected, avoided, minimized, or bypassed."

This idea that the baby exists and develops within a temporal world shared with others has serious methodological implications that should scare any researcher, who has, then, to look at just about everything just about all the time. This seems an impossible demand, and it would be if a clever technique had not been devised. In 1958, Sander hit upon the appropriate design. Why not use the infant's bassinet as a silent spy, monitoring what she and her care-givers were doing? Over the years to come, several researchers and engineers collaborated to make this dream come true. The resulting "Sanderbed" looks like an ordinary nursery bassinet, but the baby's mattress is "bugged" to record around the clock her movements, breathing patterns, and sounds.

Data from the Sanderbed have been collected for many groups of infants. One group consisted of babies who used the bed for a month after birth while they were cared for by their mothers. The mothers all had had other children, and all fed the babies on demand. The findings revealed a complete surprise. One would have expected babies, after the stress of birth, to sleep a lot. Actually, these infants were more often awake during their first three days of life than they were at any other time before their first-month birthday. They often began their postnatal life by spending an hour or two quietly alert, and then they spent considerable time awake for the next few days. Why? Sander speculates that the babies were disrupted by the birth process so that their "old" way of regulating their cycles no longer worked. They needed, therefore, to become acquainted with their care-givers in a new way. This meant that they needed to be available to the parents so that the parents could get to know them and learn to support them. After this meeting, the babies could turn to the task of reorganizing their cycles of sleep and alertness.

If this idea has merit, then we should see evidence of "negotiations" between babies and care-givers during their first days together. Sander believed in this idea so strongly that he spent years designing an experiment to test it. The experiment involved three groups of babies, twenty-seven in all, who each used the Sanderbed for a month.

Group one consisted of infants who "roomed in" with their mothers from birth. These babies did indeed quickly begin to mesh their activity-rest cycles with their mothers' cycles. They still had their underlying forty-minute cycle, but under the mothers' now external influence, that short cycle peaked differently than was typical before birth. The process must have begun to jell during the first three days, when the infants were unusually awake, for by the fourth to sixth day they began to shift their crying and other activities to the daytime hours. By their tenth day, they were settling in to a routine where their longest periods of sleep occurred within the twelve nighttime hours.

The babies in this first group showed us that they were indeed able to adapt rather rapidly to our adult cycles. They did not, however, tell us for sure to what extent they were influenced by adults; perhaps they would have achieved this cycling without any adult aid.

To check this possibility, Sander turned to his second and third groups. Both were composed of infants who were awaiting adoption. The first group lived for ten days in a hospital nursery for newborns, with its whole "package" of bright lights, and round-the-clock bustling. They were fed on a four-hour schedule and cared for by many different members of the hospital staff. They did not begin to establish a diurnal rhythm as the first group had. By their tenth day they were, in fact, most active and fretful at night—a cycle opposite to that established by the infants who were cared for by their mothers. They were definitely not becoming entrained to normal adult rhythms of activity and rest.

These babies were, nevertheless, still establishing the necessary control mechanisms to achieve a diurnal cycle. When Sander transferred them, on their eleventh day, to the care of a single care-giver, they rapidly reversed their day-night activity cycles and assumed the normal pattern of their peers in the first group. Baby girls even seemed to move right toward an advanced degree of day-night differentiation. This, Sander believed, indicated that the babies, even though they were not given particularly responsive care in their earliest days, were still trying to regulate their cycles. The very effort provoked by their stressful first days may have given them impetus to compensate, when given the chance, with a rapidly consolidated cycle.

Sander's third group supports the idea that the babies were indeed very open to establishing mutual cycles with their care-givers. He assigned these infants to the care of one foster mother for ten days and then to that of another foster mother on day eleven. The infants in this group, already used to the routines of a specific care-giver, found the switch most disruptive. They seemed more distressed during feedings on the first day of the change, and they cried more all through the subsequent twenty-four hour period.

From these studies we can conclude that infants rapidly begin to adapt themselves to a responsive care-giver. Many researchers have tried to examine which forms of interaction, such as soothing and alerting techniques, best suit newborns. They usually present their subjects with an array of stimuli separating visual, auditory, and kinesthetic stimulation so that they can get some idea about what the babies respond to the most. For example, they may try to document the number of crying babies who are soothed by a pacifier, or by gentle rocking of the bassinet, or by the effects of warm water. Or they may design their study to see what induces the most prolonged alertness. By and large, babies seem most responsive to just those stimuli care-givers most likely provide either on purpose (a gentle backrub) or unwittingly (a smiling face filled with color and movement).

Babies differ in how rapidly they can reorganize themselves after birth. And adults, even experienced ones, differ in how they support their infants' efforts during this difficult process. Often, it is hard for an adult to figure out how to be helpful. While synchronizing his or her own actions with those of the baby may, at one time, help the baby organize his patterns of sleeping and waking, at other times interfering in the baby's patterns (waking him, for example, from a deep sleep at 10 P.M. so that he will be tired enough to sleep through the night) may be an equally supportive strategy. A mother who is truly groggy in the middle of the night, and not at all prone to turn on the lights and carry on a conversation, may be more helpful than one who manages to be lively at midnight. A baby who signals his needs clearly and regularly is of course easier to adapt to than a less reachable infant. Yet, it is critically important to understand that, underlying such individuality, the general process of adaptation relies on the baby's active ability to "self-regulate."

Responsive care-givers are important to newborns geared up to coordinate their cycles with ours, but this should not be an overly awesome responsibility. Babies seem designed to fit into our designs. While the moment-to-moment interactions may not prove smooth, the dynamic relationship between babies and care-givers appears to contain a richness and an intimate appropriateness that "naturally" fosters our infants' adaptive capacities.

7. Babies as Communicators

Your baby's signals are too powerful to ignore. Like an egocentric boss, she gives her orders with loud cries, oblivious to either your plans or needs. With a brief glance or a few soft sputters, she transforms you from a tired servant into a smiling, adoring attendant. Even her appearance—her "innocent baby face"— asserts her authority as it draws you near. All this occurs without the baby's uttering a single word.

We tend to think of communication as verbal, and that is true if we consider only telephones and books. Spoken language, an evolutionary achievement unequaled by any other species, is superbly suited to communicating when the task at hand— whether it be a problem in childrearing or an upcoming vacation—demands planning and interpersonal coordination. Using speech, we can talk about the past and future, and use this information to negotiate in the present.

But communication must also serve to integrate us into smoothly coordinated groups. Continual and reciprocal emotional comments—nods of assent, grimaces of disapproval, or postures of enthusiasm—are vital to guide individuals toward consensus and a common purpose. For such goals, verbal language contains weaknesses. Speech is not a powerful way to get across messages about inner feelings. Because language is so explicit, it poorly translates immediate emotional reactions into words.

Gestures and expressions—the only communication system our nearest ape relatives use—were not forsaken when humans developed linguistic capabilities. Body language remained the primary transmitter of inner feelings. Emotional attitudes, needs, and desires can be communicated nonverbally in extremely sophisticated ways that combine gaze, facial expression, gesture, and posture. This body language provides the affective foundation for cognitive conversations. (In fact, when it is deleted, as is the case with telephone conversations and letters, painful misunderstandings frequently occur.)

All communication is not an equal blend of words and gestures. In situations that demand specific planning, such as a business meeting, verbal messages predominate; in situations in which emotional bonds are fostered, such as in courtship, nonverbal ones are focal. In terms of social structure, one might expect to find that body-language messages are most significant within the smallest, closest social unit: the care-giver and the baby. Here, the bonding and smooth meshing between individuals seems most crucial.

Since our babies are extremely vulnerable, they must depend on others to assure their survival. But, as if to compensate for their immaturity, they also are most effective body-language communicators. Their nonverbal signals, such as their cries of hunger, control adult actions. And, we adults can barely resist this language. As our babies evolved into their present immature state, we too seem to have reciprocally developed ways to monitor and to respond to baby messages. Our species, thus, came to link babies and caregivers through a continual stream of communication.

Infants do not even have to move to communicate with adults. Their looks alone convey a critical message: "I'm a baby; nurture and protect me." "Looking like a baby" is such a widespread adaptation that Konrad Lorenz, the Nobel Prize-winning ethologist, notes that all species who bear dependent young have babies with distinctive physical features.

In some primate species, the most obvious signal of the baby's status seems to be coat color. In the *Patas* monkeys, the baby's lighter shade makes him visually distinct from others and sends the message to all adults, male and female, that he must receive special consideration: the young monkey, for example, is not treated aggressively even when he emits signals that usually provoke attack. As the infant matures, his coat gradually darkens and so, too, does the tolerance of his elders. While the light-coated child's teasing play is greeted with patient understanding, the adolescent's browning coat provides no such guarantee.

Our babies announce their "babyishness" with such adorable features as chubby cheeks, tiny noses, prominent eyes, fat arms and legs, and oversized, protruding bellies. Our attention is riveted by such an appearance—a fact ignored neither by advertisers nor by Walt Disney. Even babies of other species enjoy the persuasive power of these features when they convince us to adopt them as pets.

New parents seem particularly prone to the effects of baby appearance. Such observers as Drs. Marshall Klaus and John Kennell of Case Western Reserve even hypothesize that the parents' observing and exploring of the baby right after birth may influence their later emotional bonding with the baby.

While we doubt there is an inviolable "critical period" during which exposure to a particular baby is essential if later care-giving is to be of a high quality, it does seem plausible that the earlier we meet our infants, the more open we may be to the effect their appearance has on us. At the very moment of birth, new parents typically find their babies irresistibly adorable, even beautiful.

Nevertheless, there is a problem here, for the newborn, with her red-mottled complexion, spindly legs, bluish hands and feet, foggy eyes, and shiny wet skin does not stand a chance in the "babyishness" contest with a three-month-old. Yet, parents are often joyfully overwhelmed by the perfections of the neonate. They expend rolls of film trying to document her beauty. As the prints almost inevitably reveal, they must have suffered from a lapse of aesthetic standards. Their wonder, with her oddly molded head, asymmetrical nose, wrinkled brow, and one eye that barely opens, proves to be quite unphotogenic. The ecstatic state of new parenthood must shield the parents from some of their baby's temporary flaws. The baby has succeeded in initiating her control.

Appearance is, of course, passive and silent. It seems powerful enough, however, to elicit adult attention so that a communication channel is set up between baby and adult. The baby then immediately begins to fill this channel with a variety of active, and often noisy, signals. These serve to amplify and specify the general messages conveyed by baby-ish looks.

Crying is surely the most obvious signal, and to a weary parent it may seem all too frequent. With his cries, the baby can effectively demand your attention even when the lights are low and the hour late. Moreover, through his cries, your baby supplies you with a wealth of information about his current needs. His pattern of crying seems to change with his situation, and you are often able to interpret these minor variations and respond accordingly.

The most potent crying sound, the "distress cry," profoundly affects all adults. When our babies emit this loud and long catlike wail, any adult within hearing distance immediately tries to locate the baby and relieve his distress. Parents hardly need a demonstration of the distress cry's effectiveness, but we can offer one nevertheless. An insensitive researcher once studied what happens when a tape recording of a distress cry is played next door to a new mother's room. Without fail, each of his deceived subjects raced in to investigate. We have no report of just how these upset women greeted the sheepishly grinning doctor. But we do know that *Patas* monkey mothers attack the nearest male when they hear their babies emit their species's distress cry.

While this cross-species comparison is offered only in jest, it is not completely without interest. Often, distress cries of closely related species sound remarkably alike. Yet, not all relatives comprehend the full range of the baby's messages, as the following poignant example illustrates. Should a mallard mother hear a chick of a cousin duck species cry out, she immediately swims over to offer the baby assistance. Once the cousin chick is saved from his danger, however, his troubles have really just begun. He can call a member of a related species with a distress cry, but he cannot present other signals to elicit the mallard's care-giving and inhibit her attack. The silent chick thereby becomes a target for aggression and is often killed by his savior.

Other cry patterns may not provoke such rapid responses as a distress cry can, but they are only relatively less potent. Of these other patterns, the most basic is the "hunger cry." It often begins as a soft whimper but, if unanswered, can build up to a vigorous volume as the baby rhythmically screams out his request. The baby can sometimes control himself by mouthing his fist or some other available suckable object, but often he will be silenced only by an adult's aid or, finally, his own fatigue. In some cultures, such as the !Kung Bushmen hunter-gatherers, care-givers rarely allow the hunger cry to escalate. They quell it in a matter of seconds. In our culture, we ofen intentionally delay our response for many minutes, but we still eventually respond to over three-quarters of our babies' crying episodes.

Hunger cries get their message across to us even if we decide to ignore them. While adults vary in their sensitivity, many find themselves waking up and tensely monitoring each new spasm even after deciding that they have a rational reason to ignore their baby's plea. Lactating women feel this acutely when a burst of crying stimulates their letdown reflex, releasing a flow of milk. This intimate connection rapidly becomes quite specific as the new mother learns to identify her baby's own personal crying patterns and to become more discerning about when the baby actually needs a feeding. Yet, as many a nursing mother knows, even once she has learned to gauge her baby's needs, sometimes the mere thought of the infant's hunger stimulates her physiological response.

Cries can communicate other specific messages. The "mad cry" seems to signal the baby's displeasure at the care-giver's behavior. For example, if you delay your response to a genuine hunger cry, you may hear the cry gain an "angry" quality as air is expelled more forcefully through your infant's vocal cords. This turbulent scream may prompt you to check on your baby even after you have resolved that it is now time for sleep. Should you stand your ground, your baby's vocal demands may leave you guiltily vigilant and emotionally drained.

One last cry pattern, the "fake cry," gradually enters your baby's repertoire. While it is hard to describe, it is unmistakable to adults used to catering to a particular infant. Unlike other cry patterns, this one may become a source of potential pleasure for the care-givers. It is particularly endearing when your baby uses this signal as an invitation to begin a playful social interaction.

No one is exactly sure why baby cries are so effective in eliciting our attention and controlling our behavior. Their power is so unquestioned and universally appreciated that it is hard to imagine our not having some special innate capacity making us particularly responsive to baby screams. But, we can never really separate such innate responsiveness from what adults may have already learned about baby feelings. Even if adults never heard a newborn's cry, they still would have had hours of exposure to their own crying. This may sensitize them to empathize with the baby's displeasure, which we typically assume underlies a cry.

One way to see if there might be an innate component to our responsiveness to babies' cries is to study how newborn babies themselves react to cries. In 1971, M.L. Simner collected data that seem to support the argument that our adaptive response to cries may have a genetic basis. Although newborns have naturally had very limited experience listening to cries, Simner showed that they are still controlled by them. Babies usually respond to a cry with a cry of their own, a fact familiar to nurses who care for groups of newborns. The more like their own cry, the more powerful the stimulus. Thus, Simner found that newborns got most upset when they heard a tape recording of themselves. Another newborn's cry was only slightly less effective, while a five-and-a-half-month-old infant's cry or a computerized simulation of a cry elicited considerably less distress.

Sympathy may begin with number one but, if Simner is right, it does not stop there. Even so, we may be mistaken if we conclude that babies are able to differentiate between the various cries using the same criteria we do. Perhaps newborns cry in response to other baby cries because they are confusing these sounds with their own. Perhaps their distress mounts until they unwittingly begin to add their own voices to the commotion. The more like their own cry, the more potential there is for such an "unrealistic" analysis of the situation. There is, however, one additional finding in Simner's study that is not readily explained by this "confusion" argument: female newborns cried more often in response to another's cry than did their male peers. We leave it to you to speculate why.

Even if confusion is at the core of the baby's reaction to cries, it may nevertheless provide the basis of a lifelong sensitivity to the cry's basic message. Of course, babies react differently than adults when they process this message. While they can only respond in kind, we, at least typically, first try to use more directed responses aimed at stopping the crying. We transform the cry into a social signal, taking it as a meaningful message and reacting to it with adaptive, goal-directed activity.

Because we do not rigidly interpret the meaning of the cry, crying can become a rich and varied signal. As we attempt to formulate the "best" response to each crying episode, we usually ground our interpretation in our analysis of the particular crying pattern, our knowledge of the cry's context, and our understanding of our culture's "wisdom" concerning the correct treatment of cries. The ambiguities involved in such a multifaceted interpretation are enormous. While parents have little time to become buried in deep analysis, they may spend many seconds puzzling through a series of options before hitting upon a comfortable strategy.

This decision-making process is particularly trying when our cultural training and the apparent demands of our babies conflict. Consider, for example, the perennial problem of deciding how rapidly to react to a baby's hunger cries. Not so long ago, parents were advised that a rapid response would quickly spoil the baby. This dictum was based on the following sort of scientific logic: if you respond to almost every cry immediately, your baby learns that you are willing to tend him on his own terms. Despite your best intentions to soothe him, you are actually teaching him to cry more as you reinforce crying with attention. The end result is not the desirable happy, contented infant, but the fussy, demanding baby most of us dread.

This logic is inadequate. First of all, it does not explain why babies all gradually spend less and less of their time crying. Moreover, it is challenged by many current observations. Some of the most intriguing data were collected by Mary Ainsworth and Sylvia Bell. They repeatedly observed the interaction of babies and their mothers at home during the children's first year. They noted, among other things, how quickly the mothers responded to their babies' cries. The mothers were remarkably consistent on this count. Those who habitually responded rapidly were most likely to have the babies who cried the least by the end of their first year, and who more often used other means of communicating, such as gesturing and more pleasant forms of vocalizing. Mothers who delayed responses or who responded less often seemed to have infants who more closely match our idea of "spoiled" children. Babies of responsive mothers, then, were apparently not learning to manipulate their care-givers with cries. Rather, they may have had more opportunities to develop other means of communicating during the periods of responsive care-giving that their crying called forth.

Unfortunately, not all early vocal signals have such a clear-cut relationship to adult responsiveness. Fussing, for example, resembles crying but is distinguished by its softer, less provoking quality. While "one" fuss may not have the power of "one" cry, a fussy spell can drive parents to distraction if their babies cannot be soothed by care-giving interventions. Some babies seem so immune to parents' ministerings that we have a special label, "colic," to describe their persistent irritability. Despite many well-intentioned attempts to calm such babies, they are usually not easily placated and their fussy periods seem to run their own course, declining predictably toward the end of the third month. Yet, although fussing may be a baby signal that does not immediately inspire a specific set of effective adult responses, it may serve an adaptive, communicative function. British psychoanalyst John Bowlby argues that "fussing" is an inborn method of ensuring that the parents continue to pay attention even after their feeding and other care-giving chores are temporarily finished.

The newborn's "negative" sounds certainly tell us a lot about a baby's mood. But if a baby could only fuss and cry, caring for one would be a most dreary task. Adults would be asked to soothe and minister, but they would receive little thanks in return. The "joys" of parenthood would be so elusive we might have difficulty remaining deeply committed to childrearing during the baby's most demanding developmental period.

We need not worry, however, for babies also have ways to convey their delight, ways that are as compelling as their many distress signals. Effective "positive" signals take a little longer to consolidate than the "negative" signals. Babies enter the world crying, but it will be a few weeks before they add clear coos to their repertoire. Even so, a few of their initial sounds prepare us for their later gleeful vocalizations. Adults often listen to their babies' first sighs and pleasurable gurgles as if they were meaningful. And, just as parents' minds and bodies seem about to disintegrate for lack of sleep, the six-week-old confirms their anticipations with strings of delightful "coo-babbles."

The most prized of all positive signals is undoubtedly the smile. Like the coo, it too only gradually emerges. At first, babies smile mostly during sleep or the transition to sleep. Most of their facial expressions during sleep appear to be unadultlike grimaces, but a few—perhaps one every six minutes—are unmistakably smiles. These fleeting lip curls, often mislabeled gas smiles, seem part of their general rhythmic discharging of nervous energy. The less mature the baby, the more discharging occurs. So, premature babies often seem to smile the most as they blissfully grimace during their long REM sleep periods.

Many researchers have tried to determine what makes babies smile and how they develop full-blown "social" smiles in only a few weeks' time. The answer is complicated. Part of it has to do with how the nervous system matures. Premature babies follow the same developmental pattern as full-term infants, marking time not from their early birth dates but from the date of conception. Congenitally blind infants, who never have a chance to see a smile, also develop smiles according to the milestones recorded for sighted infants.

Yet maturational development certainly does not occur in a vacuum. Babies quickly alter their responsivity to different events. While at first they seem willing to smile in response to a wide array of moderately intense stimuli (frequently favoring voices), they soon smile selectively to different events. Faces become, by three months, the best smile-provokers, especially when the babies and adults make eye-to-eye contact. Often before the fifth month, just any face will no longer do; your baby will smile most often to you. Congenitally blind babies also narrow down and specify the range of stimuli, but they are forced to use sounds and touches as clues to when to smile, and they often do not sustain their smiles as long as babies who can pick up on visual information.

John S. Watson of the University of California at Berkeley has explored the adult's role in the baby's development of social signals using what he calls "the Game" hypothesis. He argues that if babies experience a stimulus and a response occurring contingently, the stimulus gains new meaning. The meaning is that the stimulus is "social": cause for the babies to burst out in smiles and coos. To set up the Game, Watson did such things as hang mobiles above the babies so that the mobiles would move each time they kicked their feet. Sure enough, the contingency between the foot action and the mobiles' response delighted the babies.

But outside the laboratory, who plays the Game? Here, nature has set us up again, for adults are most likely to play the babies' "game." We delight in providing our infants with contingency experiences as, for example, we touch their noses each time they look up, or as we make a sound after every coo. According to Watson, the Game is not important to infants because people play it, but, rather, people become important to infants because they play the Game. The fact that a mobile can also play the Game does not, of course, diminish our importance to our babies, for in their natural environment we are still their primary sources of contingency responses.

In another way, also, adult actions play an essential role in the development of babies' smiles. While a responsive mobile may work as well as a responsive human in eliciting smiles and coos, it cannot go further; it cannot tell the babies what smiles mean. We, on the other hand, gladly transform baby expressions into social signals. Newborns make relatively few recognizable expressions—even their smiles are tentative and fleeting—yet we strive to abstract patterns from their amorphous movements, zeroing in on signals which we consider significant carriers of affective information even before our babies can send sharp messages neatly tied to our efforts. We probably base our selection on what we intuitively know about human communicative capacities. As we make these interpretations and as we respond contingently, as though the babies intended some meaning, we help our babies flourish as social organisms. We give social meaning to baby movements that the babies alone could not invent.

Our tendency to find specific social meaning in our babies' first actions and to provide predictable responses to these selected signals is balanced by our flexible approach to reading baby messages. While parents and researchers alike tend to make a great fuss over specific baby signals such as cry sounds and smiles, we are at the same time aware of a whole constellation of baby signals. The baby never *only* smiles or *only* cries. These discrete actions are always embedded in a whole "package" of movements, which we view in a specific context.

Even when we are looking specifically for a smile or listening for a cry, we attend to multimedia messages. The crying baby augments his auditory demands with visual suggestions—grimaces and heightened color—and with tactile ones—tensing muscles and flaying limbs. We then may label this "package" a cry, but because it contains so much redundant information, we can read it without hearing a sound. Thus, the baby does not have to make stereotypic displays to convey his message. He can send the same communication in a variety of packages, substituting one specific display, such as a sound, for another, such as a movement. The adult's ability to understand this process permits the baby to communicate constantly long before he makes conventional social gestures and words.

Using a common repertoire of multimedia signals, newborn infants can personalize their messages. The individuality, or personal style, babies exhibit right from birth influences others as they form their first communicative relationships.

Susan Goldberg, a psychologist at Brandeis University, has a provocative system for describing how babies' communication styles differ. Using three "dimensions," she describes how certain baby characteristics may affect adults as they try to understand their babies. Her first dimension is *readability.* Goldberg suggests that, over the course of constant interchanges, a parent assesses how clearly her baby communicates. This readability assessment then influences her judgment about what her baby is conveying as she attempts to decipher each new message. Of course, this assessment can be revised if the baby's readability is altered by circumstance or fluctuates widely, but many infants remain fairly consistent. When a parent says, "When Anna's tired, she looks more alert than ever, so we pick her up, only to find that she's fussy, so we put her down, and she looks wide awake again," he has most likely made the judgment that Anna sends out only vague or contradictory signals that he has difficulty unscrambling. But when another parent exclaims, "Daniel just winds down gradually. His eyelids droop. He turns his motor off and goes to sleep," she is saying that her baby is usually "legible."

With her second dimension, Goldberg attempts to describe a baby's *predictability.* Some babies offer care-givers consistent enough responses to certain ways of handling them that it is possible to make fairly accurate judgments concerning their effects. Others seem to "go either way." Swaddling, for instance, may calm a baby down one time, and anger him the next, or it may always provoke the same reaction. Certainly it is easier for the care-giver to understand the baby's message if the baby reacts predictably. The care-giver can then anticipate how to achieve a specific goal, since past experiences help him anticipate the future. But, if the baby is extremely unpredictable, the care-giver may find that he comes to anticipate only uncertainty.

Goldberg uses her third dimension—*responsiveness*—to gauge the quality and extent of a baby's response to different types of stimulation. This is a very complicated dimension, since both the baby who overreacts to every stimulus and one who rarely reacts to any are usually not regarded as optimally responsive. A baby who responds readily with well modulated behavior when you cuddle her presents a much different personal style than one who does not react at all, or one who reacts quickly but with a vigorous arch backward. These general characterizations are not, moreover, sufficient. The baby who overreacts to cuddling, for example, may not react so violently to another kind of stimuli, such as a noise. But Goldberg argues that parents are able to make a judgment that adequately summarizes this diversity and that enables them to implicitly place their baby on a continuum from excellently to poorly responsive.

An interesting aspect of Goldberg's dimensions is that they describe not only the baby but also his adult partner. How well a baby communicates is, of course, influenced by how attentive and understanding his adult listener is. But when any baby is unreadable, unpredictable, unresponsive, or responsive to the extreme, an initially responsive parent may be trapped in cycles of ineffective interaction that make him or her feel helpless, a failure. Parents, just like babies, may need to experience some of Watson's contingencies if they too are to "smile and coo."

This trap may be avoided if the care-givers are able to modify their approach to suit the baby's individuality. With practice, parents can learn to decipher the messages of even the most extremely uncommunicative babies, such as very young premature infants or congenitally blind children. In the former case, the infants' profound immaturity robs them temporarily of many of the means of sending intelligible messages to their care-givers. Babies born eight weeks early will not begin to smile regularly until they are almost fourteen weeks old, the equivalent of a six-week-old full-term baby. Premature babies will also cry less at first than a full-term baby, and will spend less time awake and active. Parents can, nevertheless, learn to compensate by focusing on "quieter," much more subtle behavior patterns, such as breathing rhythms, to read their premature babies' communications.

Congenitally blind infants are plagued (permanently) by atypical communicative patterns because they are deprived of the visual feedback that usually sustains infant affective expressions, such as smiles, and helps sighted infants modulate their movements. Selma Fraiberg, in her book *Insights from the Blind,* notes that it is very difficult to read the relatively unanimated sign language of blind babies. Not only are they unable to "woo their care-givers with their eyes," their care-givers often react as if the lack of eye contact means the baby is "not friendly" or "not interested." Fraiberg has developed ways to aid these parents by helping them understand the communicative content of their baby's impoverished repertoire of facial signs (for such babies, a very still face may signal alertness) and by highlighting what the baby is saying with his hands (for instance, a fleeting and light touch says, "More!"; a grasping-ungrasping movement indicates, "I want!").

The differences that Goldberg describes in baby interactive styles seem to influence parents as early as an infant's very first days. Joy Osofsky, a researcher who worked at Temple University, demonstrated this with 134 baby-and-mother pairs during the second, third, and fourth days after birth. Each baby was first assessed using the Brazelton examination. Then Osofsky's research staff observed each mother and baby in two more situations. First, they recorded how each baby and mother acted during one of their first bottle-feeding interactions. During the second behavioral observation, they recorded what happened as the mother attempted to perform some of the items of the Brazelton—having the baby turn to her voice or visually follow the movement of a red ball.

Osofsky found that the babies were remarkably consistent communicators during the three observations. Infants who were alert and responsive in one situation were alert and responsive in the others. For example, infants who could follow a face with their eyes in the initial testing tended to do so as well in the feeding situation or when their mothers played with them. The most exciting finding, however, had to do not with the consistency of the infants' style, or the mothers', but with the match-up of babies with mothers. If, for example, a baby was most responsive to sounds, then his mother would talk more to him, while if a baby was more visually oriented, his mother might talk less yet give him more minutes to enjoy her own motion-filled face.

To obtain such a predictable relationship between the styles of infant and mother, the baby and the mother must both be contributing to their interaction. The influence of the babies, Osofsky concludes, cannot be overlooked if we want to understand differences in what mothers do with them during their first days.

How the interaction between babies and care-givers develops depends, then, on both the babies' and the care-givers' communications. Because the influence is mutual and dynamic, it is very difficult to predict what will happen months or even weeks in the future. Yet, the baby may well have certain consistent ways of presenting messages so that parents and researchers can, at least retrospectively, follow how the baby became the type of interactor he or she is at the end of early infancy.

Jeannette Haviland took advantage of a relatively rare occurrence to illustrate some aspects of the infant's consistency in interpersonal style. While she was a researcher at the Educational Testing Service in Princeton, New Jersey, she gave birth to twins. For the next two and a half years, she made weekly films of Lizbeth and Alex, and she recorded the comments of visitors as they stopped by her office to visit the twins.

Haviland found that Lizbeth and Alex presented "two different faces on the world." Using her films, she could trace stable differences in the way the twins expressed themselves. Lizbeth seemed more active; she moved her mouth expressively and looked upward at the world with wide eyes. Alex's facial features were, in contrast, more often immobile; he watched the world through downward glances. But it was not just their appearance that seemed to convey their personal style. Since Alex was overall more "bland," when he did make a dramatic expression, such as a smile, he was able to command more attention and provoke more interest than Lizbeth was able to do with her more frequent appeals. Adults, Haviland concludes, probably read expressions made by babies in the context of the baby's usual behavior. So Alex, with his typically steady "ground," was able to make the most of his smiles and coos, while Lizbeth was not able to derive as much power from each individual expression.

Adults visiting the babies seemed struck by their differences. Haviland was unable to find quantitative differences in their responsiveness, since the twins performed the same on traditional infant tests. Rather, she thought that her babies' visitors were reacting to consistent differences in styles of responsiveness which they took to be meaningful indicators of who each baby was. This in turn led them to characterize each infant as an individual; Lizbeth was called such endearing names as "woozey" and "little pumpkin," while Alex earned the reputation of "a cool customer" and "the judge."

We cannot question that babies possess physical and behavioral attributes that we adults are eager and able to read. And since our responses are guided by their signals, we can even say that as babies provide us with information about their needs and desires, they assert control over our activities.

Nevertheless, we might hesitate to say that babies are indeed communicators. True communication is a back-and-forth process, and babies cannot be said to communicate in that sense until they develop ways to read others' signals and modify their behavior accordingly. Though babies emit signals, they may neither "mean" their messages nor find meaning in ours. If this is so, babies communicate only passively, even when they scream and squirm. Adult humans, the world's most magnificently complicated cognitive beings, have the ability to read meaning into newborn signals, and modify what they do based on this reading. The adult, not the infant, is the true communicator.

Recent research profoundly challenges this view. As we will now see, babies not only can control our behavior passively, but also seem equipped to interact responsively, so that you, the adult, can be a receiver of baby messages, as well as a sender of your own.

8. Babies as Interactors

New parents do not seem satisfied to assume only that their babies are passive communicators. They also often insist that their new child is a human social partner who has the basic capacities to interact with them. Just eavesdrop on a parent playing with his infant and you will hear this belief articulated. Should the baby glance at his face alertly, he will probably ask the baby a question such as, "You think I want to play, don't you?" or, if the baby grimaces and averts his gaze, "You don't like silly songs, do you?"

Until recently, researchers claimed that the beliefs implied by such scenes were baseless. No young baby, their argument typically read, could possibly enter her new world possessing the complicated talents required for true social interaction. It was only a fanciful parental pastime to read baby communications as suggestions that the baby might indeed modify her actions based on what her partner is doing. It was admitted that infants could respond automatically to certain adult cues. But it seemed impossible that babies could respect the rules of reciprocity, meshing their messages with their partners' so that they could take turns as speakers and listeners, and sharing common notions about messages like "hello" and "goodbye." Babies, especially during their overwhelming first weeks, seemed to such researchers too wrapped up in themselves to show such respect for another person's communications.

This view makes a great deal of sense. We adults are, after all, interactive geniuses who often behave as if our environment is filled with "partners" even when we know many are not really capable of reciprocity. For example, we may "read" the full moon's face and find its grin consoling or its grimace unnerving. Yet, in our culture, we dismiss such conclusions as fanciful; we can argue persuasively how we develop the capacities to "pretend" that the moon can "mean." Our motivation to believe that baby actions are communicative and interactive is much stronger and much more adaptive. An adult can anticipate what the baby will become. Just as an adult can choose to react to some facial expressions as though they were intended to convey meaning, she can set up an interactive framework between herself and the baby long before the baby can really be a partner. In this view, the new baby is as uncomprehending as the man in the moon. Adults remain the source of any and all social quality perceived in interactions with a baby.

This view gives much credit to the parent. The parent can overlook the baby's confusion and bring order into their relationship. The parent can draw the baby into human social life by pushing him gently toward reciprocal exchanges. If the first parent-infant exchanges appear to be true interactions, we should praise the parent for orchestrating a deceptively complicated "conversation." The baby will need many weeks before he can actually participate in the organization that the parent so lovingly provides.

Both theorists and researchers are now seriously questioning this traditional view. On the theoretical level, the reconceptualizations of the baby-parent relationship in terms of our species's evolutionary heritage suggests that human infants may be born prepared for the crucial adaptive process of social interaction. From scores of research projects similar challenges are beginning to emerge. Observations of how newborns first interact with other people are showing us a sophisticated infant who already seems equipped to relate to others.

Many of the daily contacts a new baby has with other human beings are focused on tasks. Most of the baby's activities, from feeding to elimination and even to changing position, enlist the efforts of a care-giver. Yet, when such tasks are completed, the baby often remains alert, ready for other contacts as well. Throughout the day, the care-giver and the baby spend minutes merely delighting in their togetherness. Such playful moments probably place the greatest demands on the communicative capacities of each partner, since no outside task defines interactions. These moments may be the proving ground for the baby's communicative understanding of his contacts with other people.

At Children's Hospital in Boston, we collaborated with other researchers in an effort to create such playful moments in a specially designed laboratory. A group of mothers and their babies visited us repeatedly over the course of the babies' first six months after birth. The baby's role was to sit in our comfortable infant-seat in a curtained alcove, and to "behave" for us. The mother was asked to enter and to leave the alcove according to our cues. As she did so, we made videotapes using two unobtrusive cameras so that we could record everything the baby and mother did. We also invited the mother to watch our videotapes so that she could share in the intriguing experience of watching her baby develop social graces.

During many of our sessions we simply asked the mother to enter the alcove and play with her baby. Altogether we taped over 150 mother-baby interactions. Each is unique. Not only did each mother-infant pair act differently together, but even the same pair played together differently during each of their visits. Yet, underlying all the individual play variations, we found an astonishing degree of order. The babies and their mothers were creating a pattern of play that was regular in its basic structure. Daniel Stern, a researcher at Columbia University who has made extensive contributions to the study of these "first relationships," aptly calls this structure a "biologically designed choreography" in which the mother and baby perform a dance of mutual delight.

The following narrative is of the first minute of a play session between one of the mothers and her two-and-a-half-month-old son, Jesse:

> Jesse is looking off to the side, sitting comfortably in the infant-seat. He cannot see anyone because of the curtains around his sides and back. He is very still and quiet; his face is serious, with droopy cheeks, a half-open mouth, and a slight down-turn of his lips. There is, however, an expectant look in his wide-open eyes as he hears his mother's footsteps. His face and hands reach out in the direction of the sound.
>
> Jesse's mother enters his alcove, smiling and saying "hello" in a high-pitched, cheerful voice. He follows her movement with his head and eyes as she approaches him and sits down directly in front of his chair. His body tenses, his eyes widen, and he begins to smile. As his face becomes more and more animated, he turns completely toward his mother and cycles his arms toward her. She leans forward so that her face is only a foot from his.
>
> Jesse's smile subsides gradually and, as it fades, he mouths his tongue twice and looks down briefly. His mother continues to talk, increasing the eliciting quality of her voice by speeding up her tempo and accentuating the first syllable each time she repeats, "Hi, come here." Jesse remains still, limbs and body tense and eyes averted. His mother reaches out and touches his legs and hips, gently moving them as she continues her verbal refrain.
>
> In a few seconds, Jesse again looks up and smiles widely. He narrows his eyes and brings one hand up to his mouth. He grunts softly and then vocalizes a more distinct coo sound. His arms and legs start to cycle out toward his mother once again. She begins to grin more broadly, talk more slowly and more loudly. She now contains his leg movements with her hands. Each time

Jesse vocalizes, his mother waits for him to quiet and then responds with her own vocalization. After his coo, her face becomes amazingly animated as she rounds her mouth into an open "O" and elevates her eyebrows.

Joint baby-mother "pseudo-conversation" continues until, after ten seconds of such play, Jesse sobers. He looks downward and pouts. His mother follows suit, glancing downward momentarily to his feet and adopting a more neutral facial expression. She lets go of his legs and he draws them inward.

After a brief pause, Jesse's mother begins to call him, trying to elicit his attention by tapping his arm and gently saying, "Look, look here again." As the first minute nears completion, Jesse glances upward and bursts into a dazzling smile. His mother again mirrors his excitement, which he expresses with outward limb movements and staccato vocalizations as well as with his facial expression.

This narrative demonstrates how rich even a minute of play can be. Each second is filled with always changing behavior patterns. Our task as researchers was to observe and then describe all these patterns, recording the choreography that captured the mother-infant dance.

First, we needed to look at all the "steps" the mother and the baby could make. Using a slow-motion videotape deck and all the patience we could muster, we wrote down all the different behavior patterns that occurred during the dance. To make our task manageable, we decided to look at different parts of the body separately (the arms, legs, head, body, parts of the face) as well as the voice and direction of the gaze. We also tried to summarize each pattern over one-second time periods, a job that was tedious but necessary to get a sufficiently complete picture of the dance.

The baby's steps were extremely varied. Even during the first weeks of life, we could reliably identify a wide range of facial expressions, limb movements, body positions, and vocalizations. As the babies became more mature, so too did their expressive abilities. The mother's steps were carefully tailored to suit the baby's perceptual capacities. Some steps were never—or at least rarely—performed when the mother was not directly in front of her baby. For example, when facing their infants, the mothers made a number of rhythmic hand movements, tapping the babies rapidly or slowly, or containing the babies' hips with both hands. Mothers made many exaggerated facial expressions that were equally "baby-modified." The most impressive was the playful "O" face, which we saw only during adult-baby interaction, and which every one of our mothers made when their interactions with their babies reached their peak.

After listing all the steps, we then proceeded to write choreographies, or rules for combinations of steps. This turned out to be a supreme challenge, because neither the baby nor the mother seemed to behave stereotypically. A mother, for example, might try to get a baby's attention with any of a number of different combinations of rhythmic vocalizations, hand movements, or facial changes. The baby also varied what he did, even when he seemed to be dancing the same portion of the sequence. Yet the match-up between the baby's and the mother's steps was not random: the mother hardly ever made her playful "O" face when the baby looked away, nor did the baby smile broadly when the mother was looking away. The match-up was not simple either. Each interactor seemed able to substitute one specific expression for another and still convey a similar message. Because of this, we had to generate extremely complicated choreographic systems.

The interactions could be viewed several ways. For example, we can look at what the baby and the mother are doing together to write a "dyadic," or two-person dance. We have found that there are at least five major phases when we view the dance this way. Each phase contains a different blend of baby and mother attention and affect. In the "initiation" phase either the mother or the baby is bidding for the other's attention with animated facial expressions, touches, or calls. In the "mutual orientation" portion of the dance, both mother and baby are facing each other, looking alert. "Greeting" is another phase, during which each partner expresses positive feelings using smiling, widening eyes, and making happy sounds. "Play dialogues" is another distinct part of the dance, for here the two partners take turns playing games or exchanging smiles and coos. Finally, one or both of the partners may initiate a "disengagement" phase by glancing away, either for a short breather or for a termination of the entire dance.

During their interaction, Jesse and his mother began their first minute by "mutually orienting" and then rapidly started their "greetings." Over the next minute, they oscillated between "mutual orientation" and "play dialogues," with only brief periods of "disengagement." They were able to modulate their exchanges smoothly, achieving prolonged periods of intense play and spending only a few seconds to establish positive contact. During many other interactions we observed between mother-infant pairs, either one or the other seemed less responsive to the partner's momentary changes in affect and attention. Yet, the order of the dance segments respected certain general rules regardless of the overall impression we had of the quality of a particular interaction. "Play dialogues," for example, never directly followed "disengagement," while "greetings" predictably came just after "mutual orientation."

Another kind of choreography can be written by focusing separately on the mother and baby. This we call the "monadic," or one-person dance; it describes the same steps as the dyadic dance, but it keeps each partner's identity, so that we can look more closely to see how the two people coordinate their phases to see who seems to be leading whom during the dance. The baby has a number of possible choreographic options, including looking away, greeting, or simply watching the other person—and so does the mother. From our analysis we began to see how the baby seems to be leading the mother as he changes from phase to phase. The rhythm of this movement is remarkably consistent from baby to baby. They seem to switch their attention toward and away from their mothers an average of four times a minute. The mother, at least in our laboratory setting, rarely shifts her attention like this; she remains looking at the baby with hardly an interruption. Though the baby, as he returns her gaze, acts as the leader, once the two are looking at each other it is much more difficult to discern who is leading whom. We could not tell who started a game, who chose which it would be or when to end it. How long a baby stays within one of the five phases, or even whether or not he enters a particular phase, depends on his mother's behavior and hers depends on his.

Despite the complex choreographies we can use to describe the rules of how babies and mothers behave when face-to-face, you might still feel that you must object. The baby need not understand any of these rules to dance along. Maybe the mother is just supersensitive to what the baby is doing. Maybe she is able to predict what he will do next and is thus able to modify her behavior while he is only able to dance in isolation. The mother then makes her baby look like a star. In fact, maybe she is such a superb dance master that only in her presence does her pupil appear to be dancing in an interactive rhythm. Take away the mother's supporting and directing role, and you might see just how inept the baby really is.

One way to force a baby to demonstrate his understanding of this choreography of social interaction is to have his mother break the rules. Rather than letting her try her best to display her baby's "talents," you can ask her to behave in a way that might trick the baby into revealing his knowledge of the dance. This is a very demanding request to make of a mother. An adult finds it very hard to submit to a pattern that does not naturally flow with the baby's. The mothers in our study were nevertheless able to fulfill our requests rather than their babies'. You might enjoy trying some of our "tricks," but, without the support of cameras and an audience of researchers, you may find it nearly impossible to sustain an experimental posture toward your baby. Such is your baby's incredible power to control you!

The most dramatic experimental manipulation we tried involved what we call a "still-faced" mother. As in the earlier situation, we asked the mother to enter the baby's alcove and to sit face-to-face before him. But in the still-face situation, she was requested neither to move nor to speak for three (seemingly endless) minutes. We found that in each case the pattern of the interactive dance was severely disrupted, and the baby revealed his knowledge of the choreography. Here, for example, is how Jesse reacted when his usually responsive mother entered with a still-face:

> Jesse is looking down at his hands, watching his fingers moving together. As his mother appears, his hands stop moving. He looks up, makes eye contact, and smiles broadly. His mother's unchanging neutral face and steady glare greet him. He looks away quickly to one side and remains quiet. His face is sober and motionless. He remains this way for twenty seconds.
>
> Jesse finally looks back toward his mother. His eyebrows arch and eyes widen as he moves his hands and arms jerkily outward. He then quickly averts his gaze, looking downward at his hands. After eight seconds, he glances at her again, this time beginning to smile with great energy. Just as his smile begins to peak, Jesse transforms it into a yawn. Closing his eyes, he arches his back and pulls in his limbs. Then, after one more ever-so-brief peek at his mother, he sobers, turns his head partially to the side, tucks his chin into his chest, and slumps over.
>
> He remains in this curled up posture for well over a minute, changing position only slightly as he repeatedly peeks briefly at his mother's face. Finally he grimaces, furrows his eyebrows, and buries his chin farther into his chest. He begins to finger his mouth, sucking one finger and rocking gently. He looks wary, helpless, and withdrawn.
>
> Jesse may still be monitoring his mother. At the end of the three-minute period, she quietly begins to leave. He immediately glances upward and follows her exit with his sober face and dejected slump.

During the still-face condition, the babies did not act either as they did when they were alone or as they did when they were with a responsive mother. Their positive greetings remained appropriate to an interaction, while their negative affect was much more profound than any we observed dur-

ing their periods alone or with their mothers. Moreover, as
the baby responded to his still-faced mother, he revealed to us
his rudimentary knowledge of the normal, social, interactive
dance. His mother was sending him contradictory messages:
by entering and facing him, the mother was initiating and setting the stage for an interaction—she was saying "hello"; by
then not responding to his "greeting," she was contradicting
her first statement by simultaneously saying "goodbye, I'm
not available for play." The infant, because of his capacity to
apprehend this message of his mother's displays, seemed
trapped by the contradiction. He too initiated and greeted.
Then he saw his mother disengaged, and he too turned away
and withdrew. He returned, however, with new greetings and
then with more rapid, deeper withdrawals. In just a few minutes, he stopped trying to initiate play; he just sat, wary and
upset. But he was still paying attention, for he knew exactly
when his mother broke off her puzzling still-face and returned to her usual responsive self.

When do such capacities begin to develop? We are not
sure, and in fact, we doubt that there is a "beginning" that we
can date with certainty. Our youngest subjects were only two
weeks old, and they, too, appeared perplexed by a still-faced
mother. Yet their abilities to express their understanding of
what they perceived were much less clear-cut than those of
babies who, like Jesse, smiled dramatically. As our babies
grew older, they became more and more determined to get
their mothers back on an interactive track. By five months,
for example, Jesse made experimenting with him impossible;
no one in the room could resist his gleeful pseudo-laughs and
pleading facial expressions. While his ability to control our
actions had definitely increased, we are not sure—and
perhaps will never know how to be sure—if his basic analysis
of our bizarre experimental condition had also changed.

The still-face condition proved so powerful a disturbance that we hesitated to continue our research plan. It
reminded us all too vividly of what many observers of hospi-
talized and stressed babies have noted—infants deprived of
reciprocity for an extended period of time may become
withdrawn and unresponsive to people. We did continue,

however, since our temporary distortion actually seemed to have produced some unexpected positive results. Mothers often commented that the excited glee of their babies the next time they entered the alcove (often less than ten seconds after their still-faced exit) was the strongest indication that they had ever had that their babies cared about what they did. They recognized the significance of their babies' active attempts to elicit positive interactions, and they seemed to find the confirmation of their babies' social understanding worth the few moments of disturbance provoked by our requests.

Other distortions that change the natural choreography of the mother-infant dance readily lead to very positive baby behavior. The typical dance, as performed in our laboratory, proceeds at quite a rapid rate even though the parent modifies her tempo to suit her baby's relatively slow rate of digesting information. You can slow down even more, however, if you consciously attempt to lengthen both your speaking and pauses. When you are interacting with your baby, slow the game down by counting out loud to ten very, very slowly. Your face and other expressive movements will naturally slow as well, as you stay in synchrony with your own vocalizations. Many babies delight in this slow-motion speech. They sustain their attention and positive affect for many seconds, often straining to fill your pauses with their own vocalizations and to move their limbs in time with your steady rhythm. This "trick" reveals just how well your baby can modify the pace of his dance in response to the pace of yours. And it proves satisfying to parents who, of course, enjoy their infants' magnificent displays of positive feelings.

The "trick" of counting slowly illustrates that babies, even newborn babies, can time their movements so that they are in synchrony with the behavior of their partners. William Condon and Louis Sander of Boston University medical school became intrigued by such interpersonal synchrony and set out to examine just when and how well babies could become entrained with the rhythms of human speech. When two adults engage in a conversation, their bodies are also in motion. Close analysis—*really* close analysis, down into the world of milliseconds—reveals that these movements are not random, even in the listener. The listener unconsciously moves his body according to the pattern of the speaker's vocalizations. The coordination is very refined, a change in posture or movement coinciding with each sound as closely as a few *hundredths* of a second.

Even more astonishingly, babies also seem capable of moving to the "vibrations" of speech. To show this, Condon and Sander filmed a group of babies, twelve hours to fourteen days old, as they moved during the playing of tape recordings. They heard tapes of adults speaking English or Chinese, as well as of disconnected vowel sounds or tappings. After filming, Condon and Sander sat, for many months, with a special projector equipped to allow them to control the speed of the film so that the images were slowed enough to examine a millisecond's movement. Each time a baby moved so much as a finger, they took note. Then they matched the time at which the movements occurred to the time at which the smallest units of sounds were heard in the words we use—phonemes such as *ch* or *mmm*. Sure enough, Condon and Sander emerged from their laboratory proclaiming that babies could move in synchrony with speech, be it English or Chinese. They did *not*, however, move to the rhythm of unnatural strings or vowel sounds or to mere tapping.

To give you a feel for the dimensions of this microworld, let us quote just a few of the details of Condon and Sander's analysis of how one baby moved to the "come" portion of the phrase, "Come over and see who's over here":

> As the adult emits the *kk* of "come," which lasts for 0.07 second, the infant's head moves [to the] right very slightly, the left elbow extends slightly, the right shoulder rotates upward, the left shoulder rotates outward slightly, the right hip rotates outward fast, the left hip extends slightly, and the big toe [yes, the big toe!] of the left foot adducts [curls]. These body parts sustain these directions and speeds of movement together for this 0.07-second interval. This forms a "unit" composed of the sustained relation of these movements of the body.

They then proceeded to note that this unit of movement during *kk* contrasted with the movements of the next unit, during the *mm* part of "come," which lasted 0.1 second.

The left elbow increases speed, the right hip adds extension, the left hip adds rotation inward, and the big toe stops moving. The previous head movement continues. . . .

The discovery of the baby in this microworld "vibrating" to such minute changes in adult speech patterns is truly remarkable. In fact, it is almost unbelievable, since it means that babies must somehow be processing events at a rate still thought much, much too fast for them. Rather than interpreting these results to mean babies can indeed process information at inexplicable speeds, perhaps we should conclude that the infants are simply moving in synchrony to the ordinary tempos of human speech, and that it is misleading to break their movements up into microseconds. This interpretation, however, makes the results no less remarkable. Little research has been done using Condon and Sander's painstaking procedure. (Few researchers are up to the demands of such detail.) But further work of this nature would truly be a significant contribution to our understanding of babies. If babies move in synchrony to speech at birth, they may well be born in harmony with the most complicated of human communicative systems. Such sensitivity to the speech of human adults could prepare the baby for the form and structure of her culture's language months before she utters her first word.

We have made one clinical observation that supports Condon and Sander's general argument. One day a mother brought her four-month-old boy to us with the concern that she suspected he was not able to hear. She had been to many other people and, since it is very difficult to test such a young infant's hearing, she had yet to receive a satisfactory answer to her question. First we asked the mother to interact with her baby, face-to-face, in our usual laboratory situation. The interaction appeared to be well-organized, as the baby and mother performed a typical interactive dance. We could not believe the baby was not hearing the mother, but we were not sure how we could persuasively demonstrate this to her. Finally, we thought of Condon and Sander's work, and we requested that the mother begin to play with her baby as before but, when we signaled, that she stop talking, continuing only to mouth the words she would otherwise have spoken. After a minute of this silent interaction, we signaled that she could resume speaking.

The clarity of the results was well beyond our expectations. As soon as the mother stopped talking, the infant ceased his interactive dance. He stared at her, made no more of his own "play-dialogue" vocalizations, sobered, and then averted his gaze. When his mother began to make sounds again, the baby immediately brightened, looked at her and greeted, and then embarked on another spurt of play dialogue. No one watching now questioned the baby's capacity to hear. And, as the relieved mother and her infant left us, we all felt grateful to Condon and Sander's work for suggesting to us how a mother's speech might provide an organizing tempo for the intricate dance between adults and infants.

By exploiting the baby's capacities to behave as a competent social partner, researchers have been able to readdress some long-standing questions about early development. These questions, though often asked about very young infants, had most often been phrased so that very young infants could not possibly answer them on their own terms. By phrasing the questions so that babies can answer them during social interactions, however, researchers are beginning to uncover some amazing phenomena that hint at a view of the infant even the most eager researcher might find incredible.

Louis Sander recently collaborated with Thomas Cassel of Wayne State University in an attempt to answer one of the most basic of parents' questions: "When can my baby know me?" In the past this question had usually been phrased by the researcher to read: "When can a baby realize that his parents are separate individuals who exist regardless of what they are doing at the present time?" When put this way, answers vary, but all clearly rule out an affirmative answer for the newborn. It takes many weeks before a baby has the cognitive capacities to understand that others retain a separate identity in time and space; and it takes many months, some say even years, before she can know someone in the adult sense. Cassel and Sander, however, rephrased the question using an interactive perspective. They asked not when the baby knows his parent per se but when he can realize that the "whole package" of his parent—her appearance and actions within a specific context—can reoccur. When does the baby, to use researchers' terminology, recognize the parent as "care-giver event"? A clever masking experiment provides the astonishing answer: within the first two weeks of life!

The masking experiment began on the baby's day of birth, as she and her mother began to establish a routine together in the hospital. Each mother agreed to bottle feed on a demand schedule, and each was already experienced with previous children of her own. On the morning of their sixth day together, when mother and baby were in their own home, a researcher visited and observed them as they went about their routine. This provided a measurement for typical care-giver activities and the baby's responses to them. Now came the "experimental perturbation." On day seven, and again on day nine, the mother went about her morning activities as usual except that she wore one of two masks and she remained silent. On one of the two days, she wore a flesh-colored mask that, except for two eyeholes, covered her face to her hairline. On the other day she wore a mask made of white gauze that was draped from a green surgical cap. Each mother wore both masks, some donning the flesh one first, the others the gauze one.

The babies not only reacted to masked mothers differently than they did to nonmasked ones, they also responded differently to each type of mask. They seemed to first recognize the change in mother-event at a particular time in the feeding routine. After being cuddled in their mothers' arms in the customary feeding position, they grasped the nipple and then briefly looked up at the mother's face. Both masks visibly upset the babies: often they changed position, and averted their eyes and faces away from the mothers' concealed faces. Once back in their cribs, after being perturbed by the flesh-colored mask, they spent more time than usual scanning the environment. When subjected to the gauze mask, babies seemed to go to sleep more rapidly than usual. In both situations, the babies drank less milk than during the normal feeding and were more often fussy or crying. Though it is difficult to interpret the different reactions to the two masks, one mother's comments succinctly summarized typical observations: "Last time [flesh mask] she kept looking and looking at me like she couldn't believe it. And she was very upset; I told you she never spit up before. This time [gauze mask] was totally different. She didn't want to have nothing to do with me. She peeked at me, then that was it. It was like a cold wind in August."

These findings suggest that the baby is indeed learning to recognize her mother during their first week of interaction. Should the mother then suddenly change, the baby can demonstrate her recognition of this fact by altering her usual behavior during their routine interactions.

A more recent study strengthens this conclusion. Babies who do not initially room-in with their mothers appear to show a diminished capacity to distinguish between the two masks and they demonstrate no changes in sleeping patterns after the masking experiments. Perhaps they will need more extensive interactions with their mothers before they become entrained to her personal interactive style.

A second problem that occupies parents and researchers alike is that of determining when babies are able to interact by imitating adult actions. Jean Piaget has argued persuasively that imitation is not a single, but a multifaceted, capacity; babies may perform certain imitations months before performing others. One kind of imitation that Piaget and many others believe exists only in the repertoire of older babies is imitating actions that the babies can see someone else perform but cannot see themselves doing, like sticking out their tongues or opening their mouths. Such "invisible" imitations, Piaget believes, demand that the imitator coordinate what he sees with how a particular action feels, an intersensory coordination that could take months to achieve within

Piaget's theory of sensorimotor development.

M. Keith Moore and Andrew Meltzoff were not satisfied with the way other researchers had tested the capacity of very young babies to perform "invisible" imitations. To really probe this issue, they felt they needed to collect films, or videotapes, of babies as they reacted to adults making a whole assortment of gestures. Then, by carefully noting exactly how babies reacted to each gesture, they could sort out if what an infant did right after she saw a certain gesture was merely a sign of interest and arousal or a specific imitation. The researchers would also have to keep close tabs on what the gesturing adult did to make sure they were not unconsciously reinforcing the baby's appropriate response in such a way that they made the baby appear more capable than she really was.

Moore and Meltzoff designed a tightly controlled experiment using two-week-old babies and four gestures—lip protrusion, mouth opening, tongue protrusion, and sequential finger movements. Sensitive to their subjects, they did not ask them to perform behavior patterns that they could not possibly make, such as broad smiles or wiggles of the ear. They kept their trials short by showing the baby a gesture for only a few seconds, then waiting a few moments for a response, and then repeating the gesture. Their findings rewarded their approach. When an adult made a specific gesture, at least some babies were able to answer in kind. Babies were more likely to open their mouths after the adult opened his, move their fingers after he moved his, even stick out their tongues after he stuck out his. Moore and Meltzoff's data present a challenge to all theorists who maintain that "invisible" imitation is an accomplishment reserved for nine-month-olds.

If such early invisible imitation does exist, what might it mean? For a parent, it is a pleasant invitation to play imitative games with his or her very young baby. You can have many minutes of fun trying to exchange tongue thrusts with your infant—whether or not it works. To the theorists of babyhood, however, Moore and Meltzoff's results are a painful reminder of how little we know of a baby's capacities, and of how much hard work lies ahead. As they excitedly observe, "We are left now with some facts in search of a theory." Not only are prevailing views of sensorimotor development challenged by their findings, but so too are our notions about what the baby is able to contribute to and learn from his daily interactions with others.

One last project also prods our interest in what a very young baby is actually doing during social exchanges. Colwyn Trevarthen, a researcher at the University of Edinburgh, has long believed that very young babies show signs of an intention to speak. To document this ability, he made detailed analyses of two-month-olds as they "chatted" with their mothers. The range of prespeech gestures and even sounds during the social animation of these babies convinced Trevarthen he was correct. For example, Trevarthen watched an infant blow bubbles during an interaction. Most of us would call this activity drooling, and respond with a quick face wipe. On the contrary, claims Trevarthen, the infant was expelling air through his mouth, and it was this air that was making bubbles. The same air, when forced through the vocal cords, will make a sound. Some of these sounds, like the *th* part of "the," are made by putting the tongue between the teeth, accumulating a little air, and then letting it go. If you make the same tongue movement—but you don't have teeth—you get bubbles. Other silent and sound-filled airbursts of the two-month-old appear to occur as the baby makes other distinctive movements of her mouth and tongue.

Trevarthen claims that during his experiments, he can observe babies making distinctive hand-waving gestures that remind him of movements adults make when they are engaged in animated conversation. For example, he observed babies raising their arms near the tops of their heads, palms out and hands open, during a greeting smile. Such a "wave" only happens during the beginning of an interaction. Even more surprising is the baby-pointing gesture he describes. Here the infant subtly wiggles his fingers, extending one as if to indicate or emphasize something to his partner. And again, subtle as the gesture may be, it tends to occur only during social interaction.

The intimate relationship between mothers and babies has always been appreciated, and researchers have seldom doubted that it plays a crucial role in babies' development during their first few years of life. Yet until researchers began to invite mothers to participate in studies of newborns and very young infants in the 1960s, they did not appreciate the babies' own contributions to their social lives. Now that we have been treated to demonstrations of our newborns' openness to social interactions, we have developed an even deeper need to chart the intricacies of their natural social world. Today, the request to join the research has been extended to fathers, who Michael Lamb, their prominent champion, aptly calls "the forgotten contributors to child development."

The omission of fathers from all but the most recent research is certainly a serious oversight. Even if we consider only our nonhuman primate relatives, we find that some fathers play very central roles in their infants' lives. While some, like the male tree shrew, tend to be hostile toward their offspring, and others, like chimpanzees in the wild, appear bored by them, a few do contribute considerably to early childcare. The male marmoset, for one, assists during delivery, prechews his babies' first solid foods, and carries his children almost all the time they are not nursing. There is also evidence that even typically uninterested or aggressive primate fathers may rise to the care-giving occasion under unusual circumstances. For example, male rhesus monkeys, who would ordinarily receive little praise as care-givers, seem to increase their nurturing behavior substantially when confronted in the laboratory with a group of motherless babies.

Considering our species's extraordinary evolutionary potential to establish flexible cultural arrangements, we would expect to find much variability in our fathers' roles. Indeed, for years anthropologists have delighted in reports of our many intriguing cultural taboos and rituals that restrict or enhance a father's contributions. Beatrice and John Whiting, two leading anthropologists from Harvard, have analyzed the wide variations in fathering across many cultures. They conclude that fathers appear most involved in childcare when their marriages are monogamous, when they live in isolated nuclear families, when they are not required to be warriors, and when their wives work outside the home.

If anthropologists were given only decade-old studies of fathers and infants in our culture, they would probably conclude that we are an exception to the Whitings's generalization. Fathers are mentioned only rarely. Indeed, in a 1,300-plus-page book, *The Competent Infant*, published in 1973, fathers are referred to—and only in passing—three times! When they did receive attention in psychological literature, it was usually to discuss the effect of their absence. Even when fathers were directly observed, they seemed to be around babies only infrequently. In 1971, a new low in father status was reached when Freda Rebelsky of Boston University analyzed tape recordings of all the voices ten babies heard for six entire days in their first twelve weeks after birth. Her fathers averaged less than thirty-eight *seconds* of talking to their infants each day! Even the most loquacious father in her study spoke for only ten-and-a-half minutes every twenty-four hours.

Rebelsky's shocking statistics must be interpreted with care. First, fathers may not have displayed for her the full extent of their care-giving involvement. Perhaps they directly interacted with their new babies by cuddling them in silence. Second, the fathers' contributions during their offsprings' earliest infancy may have been primarily through their critical support of the mother and the older children. Finally, we must not overgeneralize from a small sample of fathers observed in one place at one time. This last caution is particularly important since the rituals surrounding the father's role in birthing and early infant care have changed dramatically in the past decade. No longer is it thought medically necessary (or even desirable) to send the father off to pace in a waiting room during delivery, or to force him to greet his new child through a nursery window, nor do people treat with contempt the idea that a father might participate in infant care. The rarity of paternity leaves does, however, suggest the skepticism with which the father's active participation in infant care is still generally greeted.

Such changes in cultural context provide us with the opportunity to begin to observe how fathers might nurture newborns when given the chance. Some recent studies have suggested how rapidly Rebelsky's data have been dated. For example, Ross Parke and his coworkers watched how nineteen mothers and fathers interacted with their first-born infants within two days after delivery. A nurse brought each baby into the mother's hospital room and asked, "Whom shall I give the baby to?" Then she and a male observer watched for ten minutes, taking note of what the parents and baby did. Fathers were certainly not passive bystanders. They were twice as likely as the mothers to hold the baby, and they spoke to, looked at, and touched their infants as much as the mothers did. Only in one category, smiling, did mothers significantly exceed them. Other investigators have interviewed new fathers and found them often engrossed with their newborns. Especially after holding the baby for the first time, the fathers report a magnetic attraction toward their newborn.

Undoubtedly the transition to new forms of infant care involves very complex changes in how fathers perceive and perform their role. Moreover, changes in one role by necessity alter others, and so we will have to seek an understanding of how the entire family network provides both direct and indirect support for the new baby now that fathers are welcome in the nursery. But reports, such as Parke's, that document how eager and able men can be during their baby's first days have quickly led researchers to shift from the simple question of whether or not fathers are important to more interesting ones about the *ways* fathers are important and about the ways mothers and fathers might establish different relationships with babies.

First attempts to answer these questions suggest that a focus on the father's contribution is both warranted and necessary if we are to understand what a baby's social life is like. At least by eight or nine months, babies seem to be strongly attached to both parents. While there are many forms of attachment, researchers typically find that babies certainly do not treat their fathers like strangers. Rather, just as they do when their mother departs, they may protest loudly and seek proximity; when their father returns, they may greet him gleefully. While these observations were made in a laboratory, they have a real-life parallel in many families. When the mother and baby spend the whole day together, the father's return is a major event. By the end of the first year, the infant often fills this special moment with excitement and the magic word, "Daddy."

Although babies may be attached to both parents, the quality of these relationships may not be the same. One relationship may not be "better" than the other, and, in fact, in their differences they may provide the infant with complementary views of human exchanges. Michael Lamb and Milt Kotelchuk, researchers who began the recent surge of interest in fathering, both suggest that fathers tend to be the one-year-old's "playmate," and mothers, their care-giver and teacher. The typical father of their studies spent much less time care-giving than the mother, and, when he was with his baby, he was more likely to fill the interactions with physically arousing bouts of play. The mother, of course, also played, but her games were more likely to be lower keyed, to involve toys and to include conventional rituals like peek-a-boo. Babies seemed to respond in kind, playing joyfully with Dad and seeking Mom out when distressed.

What is the younger infant's view of his two partners? Again we are in our typical bind, since we cannot simply ask them. But in our studies of early social interaction, we did try to consult six infants when they were just weeks old to ask for comments about their relationships to each parent. While they were much too young to show us strong, consolidated attachment relationships, we believe we saw them report the same differentiation of relationships Lamb and Kotelchuk report. As early as four weeks and certainly by eight, infants and fathers engaged in more excited exchanges than infants and mothers. Mothers were more likely to contain their babies' glee with gentle touches, soft pats, consoling smiles, and calming vocalizations. Together, the baby and mother sustained long periods of affectively positive "conversations." In contrast, fathers were more apt to jazz up their babies with poking games and playful punctuations. With the father, an infant more often reached heightened peaks of excitement and, when they were very young, balanced the excitement with more sustained "valleys" of recuperative inattention. Here is a description of a few moments of play between Eric and his father:

> As his father comes into view, three-month-old Eric sits upright and becomes still and attentive. As soon as his father looks directly at him, he smiles broadly, emits a short coo and abruptly kicks his legs. His father begins an almost adultlike narrative about their favorite games. Eric watches his face intently and punctuates his stillness with short vocalizations and large, abrupt leg movements. Each time he coos, his father smiles and raises his eyebrows. Yet he does not lean forward or touch Eric until he initiates a series of rhythmic touching games by walking his fingers up Eric's arms or peddling Eric's legs. Eric obviously enjoys the play for he bursts into gleeful activity at the end of each sequence and, although he then grows still and glances downward, he quickly returns for another round.

> When Eric's mother switches places with her husband, Eric enters rapidly into a dialogue in which he says a drawn-out oh, coo, or gurgle and she responds with a high-pitched, brief phrase. His mother remains very close to him during this "conversation" as she leans forward on her seat and gently embraces him by holding her hands around his waist. She rarely moves or vocalizes suddenly or vigorously, and she carefully modulates her facial expression to reflect Eric's. He, too, does not change suddenly; his limb movements are smooth and gradual, and he remains calm and alert.

Both Eric's mother and father, like all the couples we studied, established patterns of interaction with their infant, but the tempo and range of the exchanges were strikingly different.

These observations do not tell us if the baby contributed to the way the interactions were formed or if the father and mother were solely responsible for making the baby act differently. You cannot ask the baby directly, and, if the mother or father stops interacting, the baby cannot in his first weeks demonstrate he knows they are two different people. Pictures of each, for example, do not elicit different amounts of attention. But we do have a clue that babies can be given some credit for the different relationships they are developing so early. Reciprocal interactions do not always seem to occur, even when an adult tries very hard to establish them. When confronted with a stranger, even our youngest subjects were able to tell us that this unfamiliar person was unlike either mother or father. Here is one example:

> As a strange, broadly smiling adult comes toward him, Eric stares at her. He smiles tentatively and then abruptly moves his arms and legs. Within a second, his face sobers and he begins to suck in his lower lip. The stranger sits straight-backed and makes only occasional tentative touches as she tries to initiate a conversation. Eric continues to stare at her soberly and infrequently, to smile tensely or make a soft, short coo. After failing to establish a smoothly flowing exchange, the stranger suddenly holds her finger near Eric's hands. He responds by leaning forward, and looking downward at the chair strap. Several times he glances momentarily at his unfamiliar partner and tensely smiles, but always with an abrupt ending and turning away. The stranger sits back and comments, as if to herself, "He promptly ignored me, didn't he?"

Like Eric, our other babies did not enter eagerly into an interactive dance with a stranger; instead, they spent prolonged periods soberly staring at the adult. The stranger often commented after the interaction that it was difficult to read this particular baby's messages and that the baby, too, seemed aware of their interactive incompatibility.

These studies are just a first step toward understanding how babies develop relationships with people. We need to learn much more about how babies and strangers become friends, how babies react to children as well as to adults, and how the setting in which a meeting takes place influences the baby's interactive capacities. We also will have much work trying to unravel how the entire network of the family, in all its diverse forms, indirectly influences how care-givers interact with infants. But the comparison of how babies play with mother, father, and stranger does lead to a very important conclusion—infants are not preset to respond in the same rigid way to all adults, nor are they able to react only to a specific social partner. During their early exchanges with others, they can and do begin to establish unique relationships, and they start to experience the complexity of human interdependency.

Together with the documentation of the baby's perceptual and motor sophistication, research such as we have presented adds enormously to our appreciation of the newborn's ability to adapt to human social life. The immature infant seems well prepared to travel the road toward maturity with his care-givers. Alone, he is helpless, unable even to achieve his own self-regulation. He must spend many months fumbling with objects before he masters simple skills of manipulation. But with you, he can perform as an extremely competent social partner and draw from your close relationship the skills that will ultimately permit him to travel on his own.

The richness of social interactions is in its past and future as well as its present. As the infant and her care-giver "dance" together, they are revealing the legacy of our species. And, as the baby gradually comes to recognize her care-givers and to imitate and synchronize behavior patterns, she is foreshadowing her soon-to-be-developed modes of action and communication.

9. Objects and Language

In their earliest moments, babies display qualities we all possess. They arrive eager and able to perceive and act, to rivet our attention and respond to us in social ways, to express their own uniqueness and mesh with ours. No longer do researchers wait weeks or months before we look for the arrival of a person ready to find out about the world. Of course, no newborn can manipulate a toy skillfully or thrill her parents with a story. Rolling back the calendar to fix a date to the advent of our infants' human accomplishments does not diminish the glory of their achievements by the end of the second year of life. But now we are beginning to see the continuities between a newborn's first actions and these later masterful performances. Our understanding of the path of development has changed dramatically as we realize that early moments are the key to the process through which the infant realizes her full range of human capacities.

The route from your baby's first cries and defensive swipings at a cloth to his use of conventional language and exploration of objects is dominated by interpersonal communication. Your interactions over the first two years will gradually be redirected to new goals, and your basic means of communication will shift. Probably there will not be a single moment at which you realize that these changes have occurred, but you will nevertheless begin to date them in retrospect from three major events: the first smile, the first fascination with a toy, and the first word.

Starting at birth, you and your baby are already preparing for such dramatic changes. At first, your world and your baby's are, if looked at separately, profoundly different. A baby's world is not yours, not one of objects and language, but one solely of sensations and feelings. Yet, during intimate moments of sharing, these two worlds intersect. Together you develop mutually fulfilling methods of communicating, of saying to each other, "This is how I feel and how I feel about your feelings." As you share this world of meaning, you are establishing the foundations of later development.

Once you and your baby become adept at sharing smiles, your baby gradually develops new ways of relating to the world, particularly new means of manipulating objects, new actions such as reaching and grasping skillfully. As he changes, so too do the goals of the interactions you establish together. By your baby's fifth or sixth month, for example, you will notice that you are no longer so occupied with helping your baby achieve a control over physiological demands and that your play periods are no longer devoted only to the pursuit of mutual delight. You will find that your baby displays a new fascination with objects and events that go beyond the immediate boundaries of himself and of your face-to-face play. With his gestures and vocalizations, he signals his readiness to proceed to new topics, to convey the new message, "This thing over here is what we should explore and communicate about."

In our laboratory studies of face-to-face social interaction, we found that our attempts to videotape adults and babies engaging in face-to-face play became increasingly unsuccessful as the baby neared the middle of the first year. The babies seemed impatient with our arrangement. While they could not yet extricate themselves from their special infant-seats, they did their best to signal such desires in all the ways they could muster. They turned their attention to any available object, be it the chair strap or the mother's hand, as this brief scene illustrates.

Eloise glances up briefly as her mother moves in before her and sits down. Her lips curl into a small smile which is but a pale reflection of her mother's expressive greeting. Within a second, Eloise returns her gaze to the small pom-pom that hangs down from her dress. As her mother attempts to engage her attention with a barrage of prolonged name calling, Eloise seems to increase her sober absorption in the object. Her mother leans forward and tilts her head to gain a face-to-face orientation with Eloise, who still doesn't respond. Then her mother reaches to finger the pom-pom and Eloise focuses her attention on her mother's hand. After rubbing it for a few seconds, she glances up for a second, makes eye contact with her smiling mother, and then returns to exploring her dress.

This new state of affairs put a burden on our obliging adult subjects. We were asking them to play with their babies as they had in the previous sessions, but now their babies were refusing. Despite valiant efforts, many mothers could not elicit the prized smile from their preoccupied infants. They told us that they now had new ways of sharing with their babies. They were willing to take cues from their babies so that their definitions of play were expanding along with the baby's expanding horizons.

As your interactions change to incorporate new goals, such as the mutual exploration of objects, you and your baby do not suddenly abandon your earlier ways of relating. Rather, you gradually alter the old to make way for the new. Your help is of utmost importance, since alone your baby cannot gain a sense of what objects "mean" in human life. As your baby increasingly becomes an eager pupil, you increasingly take on a teaching role, as illustrated by the following scene.

Paul is looking carefully at his doll, fingering its nose. His mother sits down in front of him and softly says, "Paul, you like the dolly?" He glances up to meet her gaze for a moment but then returns soberly to his toy. His mother looks at the doll's face and reaches out to tap its nose with her finger. Paul smiles, looks up to her face and says "ta." His mother grins and then taps his nose gently. Paul babbles "ta, ta, ta" expressively and then he smiles broadly and grabs rather roughly for his mother's nose. She reacts with a gleeful, "I'll get the dolly's nose" and Paul follows her finger movement toward the doll, babbling "ta, ta, ta" once again. As soon as Paul stops vocalizing, his mother taps the doll's nose three times while saying, "tap, tap, tap, and now let's get her toes." Together they continue this object-focused game, comparing their toes, hands, and cheeks with the doll's.

Jerome Bruner suggests a helpful image to describe this very special teaching role. As your baby develops new interests, you continue to provide the "stabilizing scaffold" on which the infant can build an understanding of communication. You have some rich material to use: the foundations of affective reciprocity and a general blueprint of human ways of communicating. Thus, your teaching remains embedded in what went before and you construct a series of "scaffolds," such as the rituals of peek-a-boo and picture-book "reading," that subtly blend newly important objects into previously established patterns of face-to-face play.

In a few months, you will begin to notice that the procedures of communication once again change. Not only objects and events but also the words for them start to become focal. These words are embedded within the games you and your baby play; only gradually do they develop an existence of their own. At times you will even feel as if you are your baby's translator because only you have the rich store of experience necessary to isolate the first words from the stream of nonverbal communication you use as you play.

After four months' experience playing the "tapping game" with his mother, Paul attempts to engage his favorite baby-sitter, Kathrine, in the routine. He cheerfully reaches forward, taps her nose, and says, "Tap no, tap no." Although Kathrine smiles, bemused, she does not respond as Paul anticipated. He sobers and withdraws his hand; she tries to console him by saying "Yes, tap, it's okay." Paul whimpers softly and, when his mother turns to see what is happening, she immediately realizes the misunderstanding. She translates the words for Kathrine: "Tap your nose, and now your toes." Using this information as a guide, Kathrine then initiates a new game based on Paul's familiar theme.

With words, your baby's world and yours seem to grow even closer. By now, your meetings seem to be indisputably human. Your baby has made major strides along his developmental path. You, too, have changed. M.A.K. Halliday, a psycholinguist, argues, as we do, that what precedes language is central to it, that as adults rear their babies they "essentially go through the process of mental development all over again, but this time in the child's persona under impetus from the child." And, he adds, they are "creating a world of meaning along with him."

No single sequence of steps can describe how babies and care-givers create a world of human meaning. A rigid program could not possibly provide our young with the experiences they need to live in a fluid and complex society. Only by stepping back to survey the course of development can we see its universal outlines. The closer we move toward each baby, the more we must appreciate how we personalize development through a process deeply rooted in intimacy.

Such an individualized path of development does place special demands on us. There will always be stretches in each infant's life where the road becomes difficult for the baby and her parents to negotiate. But the difficulties are almost always met and transcended as babies and adults draw from their magnificent adaptive capacities and particular strengths.

There are, nevertheless, situations that place enormous strains on the developmental process. Over the past years, we have worked with T. Berry Brazelton and Heidelise Als to try to understand better how care-givers and babies develop communication systems to support development, despite major obstacles, over the first years. Blindness seemed to us to be a particularly acute problem: we thought that if communication lies at the heart of human existence, human beings deprived of so major a way of picking up information from others would face special dilemmas as care-givers and as infants.

In 1973, we had the rare opportunity to observe the development of a sighted baby, Mary, who was born to blind parents. We first met the parents five days after Mary's birth and they graciously agreed to let us visit them many times during the next year. We spent about one day a month with them until Mary's first birthday, videotaping care-giving activities, setting up face-to-face interactions in order to obtain observations comparable to the ones we had made in our laboratory between sighted parents and babies, and discussing how the parents monitored what their baby was doing.

The mother, a strong, warm person in her early twenties, became blind as a newborn. Her lack of sight greatly affected her interactive behavior. She rarely turned her face directly toward her partner and, since her eyes were never fully opened or expressive, her face lacked animation. Despite these major deficits in communicative behavior, she was aware of, and involved in, many intimate social relationships.

The father's interactive behavior was less atypical. He had been sighted until the age of eight and then partially sighted until he was eighteen, so he retained many of the mannerisms of seeing people. During social interactions, he adjusted his body and face appropriately toward his partner and his face was dynamic and expressive. Even so, he was not always able to mesh his interactive gestures smoothly with those of his partner.

Mary was a very attractive, healthy newborn, who was vigorous from the start. She loudly demanded her care, yet she complemented this with impressive social capacities. She was able to maintain prolonged alert periods and she cuddled irresistibly in adult arms.

During the first weeks, Mary and each of her parents

established their own unique ways of interacting. Although her father could not respond contingently to each of Mary's facial expressions, he did attract her attention quickly in face-to-face play. Once he sat directly opposite her and drew her attention to himself by speaking. He perceived when she was looking at him (reportedly by monitoring the direction of her breathing), and he filled these moments of attention with soft songs and playful kisses. When Mary turned away, he adjusted the rate of his speech, speeding up to attract her attention again, and then readjusting her position so she faced him. Through his sensitive modifications of his own behavior, he was able to maintain long periods of playful exchange.

Mary and her mother took longer to establish a comfortable way of relating, but when they did it was mutually satisfying, even though it was initially atypical. When we watched the mother we soon saw that she rarely faced her baby. To burp her, she turned her outward or prone on her lap; when she positioned Mary on her shoulder, the mother turned her face in the opposite direction or looked straight ahead. Even when she was speaking, her face remained bland and unanimated. The mother also had difficulty gauging an appropriate interactive distance so that she often sat too far away from Mary.

It took us some time to appreciate Mary's contribution to establishing a mutually satisfying way of communicating with her mother. Slowly we realized that, while she actively looked toward us and her father, she was actively averting her gaze from her mother's face. She turned her eyes and head away, moving into and maintaining awkward positions. Even when her mother did attempt to turn the infant's head toward her, Mary would tense her neck and resist the movement, shut her eyes and rapidly turn away.

By the baby's third week, her mother was well aware that Mary preferred not to look at her and she made various attempts to overcome this aversion. By clapping her hands near her own face, she tried to draw Mary's visual attention; by touching and adjusting, she tried to tease her gaze. Yet only when looking away did Mary seem relaxed enough to attend to all her mother's sensitive nonvisual messages.

Finally, Mary and her mother developed the means of successful interaction by creating their own non-face-to-face positions. Their favorite one was when the baby faced outward while seated on her mother's lap, her back supported against her mother's chest and stomach. In this position, the mother maintained tactile contact with Mary by playing games with her fingers and rhythmically patting her body. She also began vocal burst-pause games in which she would say something and wait patiently for her baby's coo.

Many problems remained but the basic solution had been found. In spite of the fact that Mary rarely looked at her mother and, thus, did not develop visual signals to convey her affective involvement with her, and even though she did not smile to her mother until she was twenty weeks old, they did share mutually pleasurable rituals of play using tactile and vocal messages.

Although their first interactions were unique in that they were not face-to-face, Mary and her mother built an affective foundation to support later developing interactions. The most critical change in their social exchanges came as objects were incorporated into their reciprocal vocal and tactile games. Mary's mother encouraged her interest in objects and derived great pleasure from her child's new skills. Two observations illustrate how crucial objects became in structuring the mother-infant interaction by the end of the first year.

The first took place when Mary was sitting on her mother's lap in their favorite non-face-to-face position. The mother focused Mary's attention on a "busy box" toy. They played a rhythmic game using various parts of the toy. At the end of a pattern, the infant would pause, then arch, turn around, and smile briefly at the mother while looking up at her face. The infant would then reorient her body forward and gaze back at the toy, patting it and vocalizing until the cycle began again. Thus, infant visual behavior had now effectively become part of their interaction.

The second observation illustrates how the patterns, first tactile, then with objects, became an important means of communicating specific information to the infant. We had asked the mother to try to get Mary to tap blocks together, a difficult task for a seven-and-a-half-month-old. The mother, facing Mary, began by playing a ritualized game of pat-a-cake. Mary responded gleefully, smiling and participating as her mother moved her hands through the familiar movements. The infant looked alternately at their joined hands, at the mother's face, and at us. Having gone through the pattern once, the mother repeated it, this time placing the blocks in the infant's hands as she moved them in rhythm with the song. The pattern was repeated once again with the blocks in the infant's hands, the mother singing and repeating the actions without actually touching the infant. Mary's attention was focused more and more closely on the blocks, the tapping guided by the familiar, pleasurable game.

Such successful interactions indicate clearly that Mary and her mother were able to establish effective communication systems that could support development in spite of a severe perturbation of usual modes of exchange. Faces usually provide the focus of a baby's attention during early interactions, but if the face is disturbingly unresponsive, a baby can alter the pattern she is so well equipped to follow by turning away, cutting off the visual channel. This allows her to free her attention and receive her mother's other messages. The process at first appears to cost dearly, but it proves beneficial, with the infant and mother establishing the basic foundations to support the infant's development as her world expands to include objects as well as responsive people. The mother's warmth and responsiveness are conveyed in many nonvisual ways so that she is able to draw her infant into a variety of interactive experiences.

Adult blindness robs a baby and care-giver of a major channel of communication. But this distortion alone does not deprive them of many other channels for establishing human connections. When, however, it is the baby who is blind from birth, the situation is extraordinarily difficult. Now the insult to our preadapted, open interactive system is multifaceted. The parents are understandably grief-stricken and if other difficulties are suspected, may have to cope for many months with uncertainty about the baby's basic potentials. The baby at birth has only a meager repertoire of behavior patterns to attract the parent. Her inability to visually explore her surroundings not only constitutes a missing channel of interaction but may also, as Selma Fraiberg suggests, convey a negative message of "no interest" and "not friendly." The gap between the baby's world and the adult's is widened, for she is deprived of her primary sensory link to both human beings and to objects.

In 1975, we began to study the development of an infant, Katie, who was blind. Despite the shock surrounding her unexpected disability, her parents were eager to mobilize their strengths immediately after birth and were willing to become involved in our year-long series of observations.

On her first Brazelton examination three days after her birth, Katie performed well within the normal limits. She was vigorous and active and was able to attend alertly to sounds. Unable to see, and thus to attend to visual displays, she appeared to have difficulty remaining calm and alert, but when she became upset she did attempt to listen and consoled herself by sucking on her fist.

By her tenth day, Katie was able to stay still and listen to sounds. But her face remained neutral and bland, and it was difficult to know whether or not this stillness was a message that she was open for interaction. Her mother did, however, try to penetrate her immobility by calling her name repeatedly in an accentuated, drawn-out song and by touching her softly. The mother summarized her attempts by saying, "A blind child can't fix and hold her attention; I have to do that for her." Katie was, thus, surrounded with a supportive emotional ambience, which allowed her to begin to develop her own ways of reciprocating.

By three weeks, Katie and her mother were enjoying brief moments of reciprocal interaction. Katie's original periods of stillness now were differentiated into moments of neutral attention and moments of brightening and movement. Katie's mother had been able to interpret her daughter's behavior sensitively enough to know when Katie was accessible and when she was not, despite the paucity of the usual signals.

The next period was nevertheless very difficult. Katie's initial abilities to remain alert and still were disintegrating by the age of about two months, and her jerky, almost continuous movements made interactive sequences hard to sustain. Despite her extraordinary worries about Katie's development, the mother persisted and refused to read Katie's apparent inaccessibility as a signal that her baby could not develop vital human connections.

By three-and-a-half months, a new resolution was achieved. Katie could pay attention easily. She could not only remain still and listen, but she could respond with smiles and coos. The mother still needed to help her by setting the stage and by guiding her orientation, but she now also received the facial expressions and happy vocalizations that for the first time informed her of her baby's communicative capacities.

By four-and-a-half months, Katie's world expanded to include objects. Games abounded as Katie could vocalize, smile, laugh, play sound and tactile games, put a pacifier in and out of her mouth at will, transfer a toy from hand to hand, and reach for her mother's face. All these accomplishments are considered astonishing for such a young blind infant and were only possible because her mother was able to help her baby establish a stable base for exploration.

The sensitivity and persistence with which Katie's mother forged a channel of communication with her daughter and then built from it a context of meaning for objects and language is extraordinary. But the basic pattern is universal. Our organization as human beings provides us with the basic building blocks of behavior which make this process quite predictable and pleasurable. But it also gives us a range of options so broad that with skill, patience, and care we can create new ways of conveying fundamental human meanings and of establishing necessary and flexible interpersonal bonds.

Babies develop these bonds with others so that they can develop socially and cognitively among other humans. Our babies begin their lives as human beings, as people eager and able to share intimate human relationships. Using their rudimentary capacities to act, perceive, and communicate, they draw from their social encounters with responsive care-givers meaningful lessons which help them understand who they are and what their world is like. As infants' capacities to manipulate objects and use language expand, so do their capacities to engage in more complex forms of human inter-dependence. Gradually over the first years, babies are eased toward becoming more fully human.

Why such fuss about a *human* newborn? Why has it been necessary for so many researchers to spend so many hours to strike upon such an obvious theme? Basically, we were looking the wrong way. Our traditional theoretical orientations led us to observe babies in isolation from their social partners and to dwell on the problem of how sophisticated adults make them into social beings. The revolutionary insight was to put babies back into their natural context—to view them as new human beings with an evolutionary heritage of social interdependency and as social people who already possess the ability to influence and be influenced by others. Within this new perspective, researchers then had to struggle to find the right method of posing the relevant questions to a baby human who has yet to master the achievements of object manipulation and language.

Although we think we can already see the bare outlines of how our adult world of objects and language is woven into the fabric of a baby's earliest social interdependency, it is too soon to assess the full impact of this new theme on our understanding of human development. Each new clue our babies provide fuels our efforts to ask them more precise questions about their perceptual, cognitive, and social capacities. In the next several years, we look forward to many exciting discoveries about our babies' abilities.

We will see many attempts to increase the scope of our understanding. Whether we are researchers or parents—or both—underlying all our specific goals is the basic aim of developing our babies' social and cognitive potentials. Studying and raising our babies can reveal our core commitment to and capacity for human interdependency. It exposes the heart of our potential and the vitality of our species. We cannot know our cultural futures, and, in years to come, the stresses to our established systems will undoubtedly be enormous. Our infants, in their dependent, immature state, must be our guides to this future.

References

1. Introducing the Baby Human

Adamson, L., and Tronick, E. 1977. Infant defensive reactions to visual occlusion. Paper presented to the Society for Research in Child Development, New Orleans 1977.

Als, H. The newborn communicates. 1977. *Journal of communication* 27:66-73.

Bower, T.G.R. 1979. *Human development.* San Francisco: W.H. Freeman.

Emde, R., and Robinson, J. 1979. The first two months: recent research in developmental psychobiology and the changing view of the newborn. In J. Noshpitz (ed.), *Basic handbook of child psychiatry 1.* New York: Basic Books.

James, W. *The principles of psychology.* 1890. New York: Henry Holt.

Kaye, K., and Brazelton, T.B. 1971. Mother-infant interaction in the organization of sucking. Paper presented to the Society for Research in Child Development, Minneapolis.

Peiper, F. 1963. *Cerebral function in infancy and childhood.* New York: Consultants Bureau.

Piaget, J. 1952. *The origins of intelligence in children.* New York: International Universities Press.

Thoman, E.; Barnett, C.; and Leiderman, P. 1971. Feeding behaviors of newborn infants as a function of parity of the mother. *Child development* 42:1471-83.

2. Your Baby's Heritage

Caudill, W. 1972. Tiny dramas: vocal communication between mother and infant in Japanese and American families. In *Mental health research in Asia and the Pacifica 2: transactional research in mental health,* ed., W.P. Lebra. Honolulu: University of Hawaii Press.

Dekaban, A. 1970. *Neurology of early childhood.* Baltimore: Williams and Wilkins Co.

Fishbein, H. 1976. *Evolution, development, and children's learning.* Pacific Palisades, CA: Goodyear Publishing Co.

Gibson, K.R. 1970. The sequence of myelinization in the brain of *macca mulatto.* Unpublished doctoral dissertation, University of California, Berkeley.

Goodman, M., and Tashian, R.E., eds. 1976. *Molecular Anthropology.* New York: Plenum Press.

Howells, W. 1973. *The evolution of the genus Homo.* Reading, MA: Addison-Wesley.

Isaac, G., and Leakey, R. 1979. *Human ancestors: readings from* Scientific American. San Francisco: W.H. Freeman and Co.

Kohler, W. 1925. *The mentality of apes.* London: K. Paul, Trench, Trubner & Co.

Konner, M. 1977. Infancy among the Kalahari Desert Sun. In *Culture and infancy: variations in the human experience,* eds. P. Leiderman, S. Tulkin, and A. Rosenfeld, New York: Academic Press.

Lee, R., and Devore, I. 1968. *Symposium on man the hunter.* Chicago: Aldine.

Lee, R., and Devore, I., eds. 1976. *Kalahari hunters and gatherers: studies of the Kung San and their neighbors.* Cambridge, MA: Harvard University Press.

Minkowski, A., ed. 1967. *Regional development of the brain in early life.* Philadelphia: F.A. Davies Co.

Montagu, A. 1965. *The human revolution.* Cleveland: World Publishing Co.

Simons, E.L. 1977. Ramapithecus. *Scientific American* 236:28-35.

Spitz, R.A. 1945. Hospitalism: an inquiry into the genesis of psychiatric conditions in early childhood. *The psychoanalytic study of the child.* 1:53-74.

Sterman, M.B.; McGinty, D.; and Adinolfi, A.; eds. 1971. *Brain development and behavior.* New York: Academic Press.

Tanner, J.M. 1962. *Growth at adolescence, with a general consideration of the effects of heredity and environmental factors upon growth and maturation from birth to maturity.* Oxford: Blackwell.

Washburn, S. 1960. Tools and human evolution. *Scientific American* 203:62-75.

3. Baby Movements

Adamson, L., and Tronick, E. 1977, see reference chapter 1.

Blauvelt, H., and McKenna, J. 1961. Mother-neonate interaction: capacity of the human newborn for orientation. In *Determinants of infant behavior,* 1: ed. B.M. Foss. New York: Wiley.

Bower, T.G.R. 1979, see reference chapter 1.

Brazelton, T.B. 1956. Sucking in infancy. *Pediatrics* 17:400-404.

Brazelton, T.B. 1973. *Neonatal behavioral assessment scale, clinic in developmental medicine* 50. Philadelphia: J.B. Lippincott.

Brown, J.V. 1973. Nonnutritive sucking in great ape and human newborns: some phylogenetic and ontogenetic characteristics. In *Fourth symposium on oral sensation and perception: development in the fetus and infant,* ed. J.F. Bosma. Washington, D.C.: U.S. Government Printing Office.

Bruner, J. 1968. *Processes of cognitive growth: infancy, Heinz Werner lecture series* 3. Worcester, MA: Clark University Press.

Butterfield, E., and Siperstein, G. 1972. Influence of contingent auditory stimulation upon nonnutritional suckle. In *Third symposium on oral sensation and perception: the mouth of the infant,* ed. J.F. Bosma. Springfield, IL: Charles C. Thomas.

Dennis, W. 1932. The role of mass activity in the development of infant behavior. *Psychological Review* 39:593-95.

Dennis, W. 1934. A description and classification of the responses of the newborn infant. *Psychological Bulletin* 31:5-22.

Gesell, A. 1945. *The embryology of behavior: the beginnings of the human mind.* New York: Harper & Brothers.

Halverson, H. 1944. Mechanisms of early infant feeding. *Journal of Genetic Psychology* 64:185-223.

Irwin, O. 1932. The organismic hypothesis and differentiation of behavior: 2. The reflex arc concept. *Psychological Review* 39:189-202.

Irwin, O. 1933. Dennis on mass activity: a reply. *Psychological Review* 40:215-19.

Jensen, K. 1932. Differential reactions to taste and temperature stimuli in newborn infants. *Genetic Psychology Monographs* 12:361-479.

Kalnins, I., and Bruner, J.S. 1973. The coordination of visual observation and instrumental behavior in early infancy. *Perception* 2:307-14.

Kessen, W.; Haith, M.; and Salapatek, P. 1970. Human infancy: a bibliography and guide. In *Carmichael's manual of child psychology* 1. 3rd ed. New York: Wiley.

Konner, M. 1976. Maternal care, infant behavior and development among the !Kung bushman. In *Kalahari hunters-gatherers: studies of the !Kung San and their neighbors,* eds. R. Lee and I. Devore, Cambridge, MA: Harvard University Press.

McGraw, M.B. 1945/1962. *The neuromuscular maturation of the human infant.* New York: Hafner Press (Macmillan).

Parmelee, A., and Michaels, R. 1971. Neurological examination of the newborn. In *Exceptional Infant* 2, ed. J. Hellmuth. New York: Brunner/Mazel.

Peiper, F. 1963, see reference chapter 1.

Pratt, K. 1934. Specificity and generalization of behavior in newborn infants: a critique. *Psychological Review* 41:265-84.

Prechtl, H.F.P. 1965. Problems of behavioral studies in the newborn infant. In *Advances in the study of behavior* 1, eds. D.S. Lehrmann, R.A. Hinde, and E. Shaw. New York: Academic Press.

Richter, C. 1931. The grasping reflex in the new-born monkey. *American Medical Association archives of neurology and psychiatry* 26:784-90.

Robinson, L. 1891. Darwinism in the nursery. *Nineteenth Century* 30:831-842

Robinson, L. 1891. Infantile atavism: being some further notes on Darwinism in the nursery. *British Medical Journal* 2:1226-27.

Robinson, R. 1969. Cerebral hemisphere function in the newborn. In *Brain and early behavior,* ed. R. Robinson. New York: Academic Press.

Sameroff, A. 1968. The components of sucking in the human newborn. *Journal of Experimental Child Psychology* 6:607-23.

Sherrington, C. 1906. *The integrative acting of the nervous system.* New Haven: Yale University Press.

Siqueland, E., and Lipsitt, L. 1966. Conditioned head-turning in human newborns. *Journal of Experimental Child Psychology* 3:356-76.

Stone, L.J.; Smith, H.T.; and Murphy, L.B., eds. *The competent infant—research and commentary.* New York: Basic Books.

Taft, L., and Cohen, H. Neonatal and infant reflexology. In *Exceptional infant* 1, ed. J. Hellmuth. Seattle: Special Child Publications.

Vollmer, H. 1958. A new reflex in young infants. *American Medical Association Journal of Diseases in Children* 95:481-84.

Watson, J., and Watson, R. 1921. Studies in infant psychology. *Scientific Monthly* 13:493-515.

Zelazo, P.; Zelazo, N.; and Kolb, S. 1972. "Walking" in the newborn. *Science* 176:314-15.

4. Baby Perceptions

Adamson, L. 1977. Defensive reactions to visual and tactile barriers during early infancy. Unpublished doctoral dissertation, University of California, Berkeley.

Ando, Y., and Hattori, H. 1969. Effects of intense noise during fetal life upon postnatal adaptability. *The Journal of the Acoustical Society of America* 47:1128-30.

Aronson, E., and Rosenbloom, S. 1971. Space perception in early infancy: perception within a common auditory-visual space. *Science* 172: 1161-63.

Ball, W., and Tronick, E. 1971. Infant responses to impending collision: optical and real. *Science* 171:818-20

Bond, E. 1972. Perception of form by the human infant. *Psychological Bulletin,* 77:225-45.

Bornstein, M.; Kessen, W.; and Weiskopf, S. 1976. The categories of hue in infancy. *Science* 191:201-202.

Bower, T.G.R.; Broughton, J.; and Moore, K. 1970. Infant responses to approaching objects: an indicator of response to distal variables. *Perception and Psychophysics,* 9:193-96.

Bower, T.G.R.; Broughton, J.; and Moore, K. 1970. The coordination of visual and tactual input in infants. *Perception and Psychophysics* 8:51-53.

Brazelton, T.B.; Scholl, M.; and Robey, J. 1966. Visual responses in the newborn. *Pediatrics* 37:284-90.

Carpenter, G.C. 1974. Mother's face and the newborn. *New Scientist* 61:742-44.

Carpenter, G.C.; Tecce, J.; Stechler, G.; and Friedman, S. 1970. Differential visual behavior to human and humanoid faces in early infancy. *Merrill-Palmer Quarterly* 16:91-108.

Crook, C., and Lipsitt, L. 1976. Neonatal nutritive sucking: effects of taste stimulation upon sucking rhythm and heart rate. *Child Development* 47:518-22.

Dayton, G.; Jones, M.; Aiu, P.; Rawson, R.; Steele, B.; and Rose, M. 1964. Developmental study of coordinated eye movements in the human infant: I. Visual acuity in the human newborn. *Archives of Ophthalmology* 71:865-70.

Eimas, P. 1975. Speech perception in early infancy. In *Infant Perception: from sensation to cognition,* 2, eds. L. Cohen and P. Salapatek. New York: Academic Press.

Eisenberg, R. 1976. *Auditory competence in early life: the roots of communicative behavior.* Baltimore: University Park Press.

Engen, T.; Lipsitt, L.; and Kaye, H. 1963. Olfactory responses and adaptation in the human neonate. *Journal of Comparative and Physiological Psychology* 56:73-77.

Fantz, R.L. 1967. Visual perception and experience in early infancy: a look at the hidden side of behavior development. In *Early behavior: comparative and developmental approaches,* eds. H. Stevenson, E. Hess, and H. Rheingold. New York: Wiley.

Fantz, R.L.; Ordy, J.; and Udelf, M. 1962. Maturation of pattern vision in infants during the first six months. *Journal of Comparative and Physiological Psychology* 55:907-17.

Gesell, A.; Ilg, F.; and Bullis, G. 1949. *Vision, its development in infant and child.* New York: P.B. Hoeber.

Goren, C.; Sarty, M.; and Wu, P. 1975. Visual following and pattern discrimination of face-like stimuli by newborn infants. *Pediatrics* 56:544-49.

Gorman, J.; Cogan, D.; and Gellis, S. 1957. An apparatus for grading the visual acuity of infants on the basis of opticokinetic nystagmus. *Pediatrics* 19:1088-92.

Haber, R., and Hershenson, M. 1973. *The psychology of visual perception.*

New York: Holt, Rinehart, and Winston.

Haith, M. 1973. Visual Scanning in newborn and young infants. In *Neurological and behavioral development of the fetus and newborn,* BIS Conference Report 29:17-23, 3ds. A. Parmelee and D. Schneider.

Haynes, H.; White, B.; and Held, R. 1965. Visual accommodation in human infants. *Science* 148:528-30.

Hershenson, M.; Kossen, W.; and Musinger, H. 1967. Ocular orientation in the human newborn infant: a close look at some positive and negative results. In *Models for perception of speech and visual form,* ed. W. Wathen-Dunn. Cambridge, MA: MIT Press.

Johnson, P., and Salisbury, D. 1975. Breathing and sucking during feeding of the newborn. In *Parent-infant interaction,* ed. M. Hofer. Amsterdam: Elsevier.

Kessen, W.; Salapatek, P.; and Haith, M. 1972. The visual response of the human newborn to linear contour. *Journal of Experimental Child Psychology* 13:9-20.

Korner, A., and Thoman, E. 1970. Visual alertness in neonates as evoked by maternal care. *Journal of Experimental Child Psychology* 10:67-78.

Ling, B. 1942. A genetic study of sustained visual fixation and associated behavior in the human infant from birth to six months. *Journal of Genetic Psychology* 61:227-77.

Macfarlane, A. 1975. Olfaction in the development of social preferences in the human neonate. In *Parent-infant interaction,* ed. M. Hofer. Amsterdam: Elsevier.

McGurk, H. 1974. Visual perception in young infants. In *New Perspectives in Child Development,* ed. B. Foss. Harmondsworth, England: Penguin.

Peiper, F. 1963, see reference chapter 1.

Piaget, J. 1952. *The origins of intelligence in children.* New York: International Universities Press.

Piaget, J. 1954. *The construction of reality in the child.* New York: Basic Books.

Salk, L. 1973. The role of the heartbeat in the relations between mother and infant. *Scientific American* 228:24-29.

Tronick, E. 1972. Stimulus control and the growth of the infant's effective visual field. *Perception and Psychophysics* 11:373-76.

Tronick, E., and Clanton, C. 1971. Infant looking patterns. *Vision Research* 11:1479-86.

Wertheimer, M. 1961. Psychomotor coordination of auditory and visual space at birth. *Science* 134:1692.

Wolff, P., and White, B. 1965. Visual pursuit and attention in young infants. *Journal of the American Academy of Child Psychiatry* 4:473-84.

5. Babies as Individuals

Als, H. 1978. Assessing an assessment: conceptual considerations, methodological issues, and a perspective on the future of the Neonatal Behavioral Assessment Scale. In *Organization and stability of newborn behavior, monographs of the Society for Research in Child Development* 43:14-28, ed. A. Sameroff.

Bell, R.Q. 1971. Stimulus control of parent or caretaker behavior by offspring. *Developmental Psychology* 4:63-72.

Bell, R.Q.; Weller, G.; and Waldrop, M. 1976. Newborn and preschooler: organization of behavior and relations between periods. *Monographs of the Society for Research in Child Development* 36.

Brazelton, T.B. 1969. *Infants and mothers—differences in development.* New York: Delacorte.

Brazelton, T.B. 1973, see reference chapter 3.

Church, J., ed. 1966. Three babies: biographies of cognitive development.
New York: Random House.

Emde, R., and Robinson, J. 1979, see reference chapter 1.

Korner, A. 1973. Sex differences in newborns with special reference to differences in the organization of oral behavior. *Journal of Child Psychology and Psychiatry* 14:19-29.

Korner, A. 1974. Methodological considerations in studying sex differences in the behavioral functioning of newborns. In *Sex differences in behavior,* eds. R. Friedman, R. Richart, and R. Van de Wiele. New York: Wiley.

Maccoby, E., and Jacklin, E. 1974. *The psychology of sex differences.* Stanford: Stanford University Press.

Moss, H. 1967. Sex, age, and state as determinants of mother-infant interaction. *Merrill-Palmer Quarterly* 13:19-36.

Rubin, J.; Provenzano, F.; and Luria, Z. 1974. The eye of the beholder: parents' views on sex of newborns. *American Journal of Orthopsychiatry* 44:512-19.

St. Clair, K. 1978. Neonatal assessment procedures: a historical review. *Child Development* 49:280-92.

Tanner, J.M. 1974. Variability of growth and maturity in newborn infants. In *The Effect of the Infant on its Caregiver,* eds. M. Lewis and L. Rosenblum. New York: Wiley.

Thomas, A., and Chess, S. 1977. *Temperament and development.* New York: Brunner/Mazel.

Tronick, E., and Brazelton, T.B. 1975. Clinical uses of the Brazelton Neonatal Behavioral Assessment. In *Exceptional Infant* 3, eds. B. Friedlander, G. Sterritt, and G. Kirk. New York: Brunner/Mazel.

6. *Some Call It Sleep*

Anders, T. 1974. The infant sleep profile. *Neuropadiatrie* 5:425-42.

Ando, Y., and Hattori, H. 1969, see reference chapter 4.

Brazelton, T.B. 1973, see reference chapter 3.

Brazelton, T.B. 1980. The joint regulation of mother-infant interaction. In *The joint regulation of behavior,* ed. E. Tronick. Baltimore: University Park Press.

Dement, W.C. 1969. The biological role of REM sleep. In *Sleep: physiology and pathology: a symposium,* ed. A. Kales. Philadelphia: J.B. Lippincott.

Dreyfus-Brisac, C. 1970. Ontogenesis of sleep in human prematures after 32 weeks of conceptual age. *Developmental Psychobiology* 3:91-121.

Emde, R.; Gaensbauer, T.G.; and Harmon, R.J. 1976. Emotional expression in infancy: a biobehavioral study. *Psychological issues monograph series* 10: monograph #37.

Kleitman, N. 1963. *Sleep and wakefulness.* Chicago: University of Chicago Press.

Korner, A. 1972. State as variable, as obstacle and as mediator of stimulation in infant research. *Merrill-Palmer Quarterly* 18:77-94.

Parmelee, A., and Stern, E. 1972. Development of state in infants. In *Sleep and the maturing nervous system,* eds. C. Clemente, D. Purpura, and F. Mayer. New York: Academic Press.

Prechtl, H. 1974. The behavioural states of the newborn. *Brain Research* 76:185-212.

Prechtl, H., and Beintema, D. 1964. *The neurological examination of the full-term newborn, clinic in developmental medicine* 12. London: Heineman.

Roffwarg, H.; Muzio, J.; and Dement, W. 1966. Ontogenetic development of the human sleep-dream cycle. *Science* 152:604:19.

Sander, L. 1975. Infant and caretaking environment: investigation and conceptualization in a system of increasing complexity. In *Explorations in Child*

Psychiatry, ed. E.J. Anthony. New York: Plenum Press.

Sontag, L.W., and Richardo, T.W. 1938. Studies in fetal behavior: fetal heart rate as a behavioral indicator. *Monographs of the Society for Research in Child Development* 3.

Sterman, M.B., and Hoppenbrouwers, T. 1971. The development of sleep-waking and rest-activity patterns from fetus to adult in man. In *Brain Development and Behavior,* eds. M.B. Sterman, D. McGinty, and A. Adinolfi. New York: Academic Press.

Wolff, P. 1967. The role of biological rhythms in early psychological development. *Bulletin of the Menninger Clinic* 31:197-218.

7. Babies as Communicators

Ainsworth, M.D.; Bell, S.; and Stayton, D. 1974. Infant-mother attachment and social development: "socialization" as a product of reciprocal responsiveness to signals. In *The Integration of a Child into a Social World,* ed. M. Richards. Cambridge: Cambridge University Press.

Bell, S., and Ainsworth, M.D. 1972. Infant crying and maternal responsiveness. *Child Development* 43:1171-90.

Bowlby, J. 1969. *Attachment and loss* 1: *attachment.* New York: Basic Books.

Bruner, J. 1975. The ontogenesis of speech acts. *Journal of Child Language* 2:1-19.

Freedman, D.G. 1964. Smiling in blind infants and the issue of innate versus acquired. *Journal of Child Psychology and Psychiatry* 5:171-84.

Fraiberg, S. 1977. *Insights from the blind: comparative studies of blind and sighted infants.* New York: Basic Books.

Goldberg, S. 1977. Social competence in infancy: a model of parent-infant interaction. *Merrill-Palmer Quarterly* 23:163-78.

Haviland, J. 1976. Looking smart: the relationship between affect and intelligence in infancy. In *Origins of Intelligence: Infancy and Early Childhood,* ed. M. Lewis. New York: Plenum Press.

Howard, J.; Parmelee, A.; Kipp, C.; and Littman, B. 1976. A neurologic comparison of pre-term and full-term infants at term conceptual age. *Journal of Pediatrics* 88:995-1002.

Jolly, A. 1972. *The evolution of primate behavior.* New York: Macmillan.

Klaus, M. and Kennell, J. 1976. *Maternal infant bonding: the impact of early separation or loss on family development.* St. Louis: Mosby.

Lorenz, K. 1935. Der Kumpan in der Umwelt des Vogels. *J. Ornithology* 83:137-213. Translated in *Studies in Animal and Human Behavior* 1. ed. R. Martin, 1970. Cambridge, MA: Harvard University Press.

Minde, K.; Ford, L.; Celhoffer, L.; and Boukydis, C. 1975. Interactions of mothers and nurses with premature infants. *Canadian Medical Association Journal* 113:741-45.

Osofsky, J., and Danzger, B. 1979. Relationships between neonatal characteristics and mother-infant interaction. *Developmental Psychology* 10:124-30.

Hall, H.R.L. 1968. Behavior and ecology of the wild Patas monkey, *Erthrocebus patas* in Uganda, in *Primates: Studies in Adaptation and Variability,* ed. Phyllis C. Jay. New York: Holt, Rinehart & Winston.

Lorenz, K. 1970. Companions as factors in the bud's environment: The conspecifica as the eliciting factor for social behavior patterns. In *Studies in Animal and Human Behavior,* 1. Cambridge, MA: Harvard University Press.

Simner, M.L. 1971. Newborn's response to the cry of another infant. *Developmental Psychology* 5:136-50.

Spitz, R. 1965. *The first year of life.* New York: International Universities Press.

Tronick, E.; Als, H.; and Brazelton, T.B. 1979. Early development of neo-

natal and infant behavior. In Human Growth 3, eds. F. Falkner and J. Tanner. New York: Plenum Press.

Tronick, E.; Als, H.; and Brazelton, T.B. 1980. Monadic phases: a structural descriptive analysis of infant-mother face-to-face interaction. *Merrill-Palmer Quarterly* 26:3-24.

Watzlawick, P.; Beavin, J.; and Jackson, D. 1967. *Pragmatics of human communication: a study of interactional patters, pathologies, and paradoxes.* New York: Norton.

Watson, J.S. 1972. Smiling, cooing and "the game?" *Merrill-Palmer Quarterly* 18:323-39.

Wolff, P.H. 1963. Observations on the early development of smiling. In *Determinants of Infant Behavior* 2, ed. B.M. Foss. London: Methuen.

Wolff, P.H. 1969. The natural history of crying and other vocalizations in early infancy. In *Determinants of Infant Behavior* 4, ed. B.M. Foss. London: Methuen.

8. Babies as Interactors

Cassel, T., and Sander, L. 1975. Neonatal recognition processes and attachment: the masking experiment. Paper presented at the Society for Research in Child Development, Denver.

Condon, W., and Sander, L. 1974. Synchrony demonstrated between movements of the neonate and adult speech. *Child Development* 45:456-62.

Dixon, S.; Yogman, M.; Tronick, E.; Adamson, L.; Als, H.; and Brazelton, T.B. 1980. Infant social interaction with parents and strangers. *Journal of the American Academy of Child Psychiatry.*

Earls, R., and Yogman, M. 1979. The father-infant relationship. In *Modern Perspectives in the Psychiatry of Infancy,* ed. J. Howells. New York: Brunner/ Mazel.

Greenberg, M., and Morris, N. 1974. Engrossment: the newborn's impact upon the father. *American Journal of Orthopsychiatry* 44:520-31.

Kotelchuk, M. 1976. The infant's relationship to the father: experimental evidence. In *The role of the father in child development,* ed. M. Lamb. New York: Wiley.

Lamb, M. 1975. Fathers: forgotten contributors to child development. *Human Development* 18:245-66.

Meltzoff, A., and Moore, K. 1977. Imitation of facial and manual gestures by human neonates. *Science* 198:75-78.

Parke, R.; O'Leary, S.; and West, S. 1972. Mother-father-newborn interaction: effects of maternal medication, labor, and sex of infant. *Proceedings of the American Psychological Association,* pp. 85-86.

Piaget, J. 1962. *Play, dreams and imitation in childhood.* New York: Norton.

Rebelsky, F., and Hanks, C. 1971. Fathers' verbal interaction with infants in the first three months of life. *Child Development,* 42:63-68.

Schaffer, H.R. 1977. Early interactive development. In *Studies in mother-infant interaction,* ed. H.R. Schaffer. London: Academic Press.

Spitz, R. 1965, see reference chapter 7.

Stern, D. 1977. *The first relationship: infant and mother.* Cambridge, MA: Harvard University Press.

Stone, L.; Smith, H.; and Murphy, L. 1972, see reference chapter 3.

Trevarthen, C. 1977. Descriptive analyses of infant communicative behavior. In *Studies in mother-infant interaction,* ed. H.R. Schaffer. London: Academic Press.

Tronick, E.; Als, H.; and Adamson, L. 1979. Structure of early face-to-face communicative interactions. In *Before speech: The beginning of interpersonal communication,* ed. M. Bullowa. Cambridge: Cambridge University Press.

Tronick, E.; Als, H.; Adamson, L.; Wise, S.; and Brazelton, T.B. 1978. The infant's response to entrapment between contradictory message in face-to-face interaction. *Journal of the American Academy of Child Psychiatry* 17:1-13.

Tronick, E.; Als, H.; and Brazelton, T.B. 1980, see reference chapter 7.

Whiting, B., and Whiting, J. 1975. *Children of six cultures.* Cambridge, MA: Harvard University Press.

9. Objects and Language

Adamson, L.; Als, H.; Tronick, E.; and Brazelton, T.B. 1977. The development of social reciprocity between a sighted infant and her blind parents. *Journal of the American Academy of Child Psychiatry* 16:194-207.

Als, H.; Tronick, E.; and Brazelton, T.B. 1980. Affective reciprocity and the development of autonomy: the study of a blind infant. *Journal of the American Academy of Child Psychiatry* 19:22-40.

Bruner, J. 1978. Learning how to do things with words. In *Human growth and development: Wolfson College Lectures,* 1976, eds. J. Bruner and A. Garton. Oxford: Clarendon Press.

Fraiberg, S. 1979. Blind infants and their mothers: an examination of the sign system. In *Before Speech: The Beginning of Interpersonal Communication,* ed. M. Bullowa. Cambridge: Cambridge University Press.

Halliday, M.A.K. 1978. Meaning and the construction of reality in early childhood. In *Modes of Perceiving and Processing Information,* eds. H. Pick, Jr., and E. Saltzman. Hillsdale, NJ: Lawrence Erlbaum Associates.

Ricks, M.; Krafchuk, E.; and Tronick, E. 1979. A descriptive study of infant-mother face-to-face interaction at 3, 6, and 9 months of age. Paper presented at the Society for Research in Child Development, San Francisco.

Trevarthen, C. 1977, see reference chapter 8.

Index

Aborigines, Australian, social
    structure of, 21
activity
    adaptation to adult cycles of,
      104-8
    level of, temperament and, 80
    rhythmicity, 80, 94, 104
    states of, 95
    times spent in, 97-98
Adamson, Lauren, studies by, 6-9,
    62-63, 128-36, 138-39, 147-50,
    152-61
adaptability, temperament and, 80
Ainsworth, Mary, 116
Als, Heidelise, 10-11, 155-56
Ando, Y., 101
anencephalic babies, 43
animals (*see also* primates)
    communication among, 111,
      112-13
    elimination habits of, 38-39
appearance as communication,
    110-12
approach/withdrawal, temperament
    and, 80
Aronson, 67
attention span, persistence, and
    temperament, 81

Australopithecus, 17-18

Babinski response, 28-29
Babkin reflex, 96
Ball, Bill, 62-63
behavior
    adaptation for survival, evolution
      and, 14-20, 38-39
    adaptation to adult diurnal cycles,
      104-8
    brain and nervous system and,
      41-43
    communication and, 109-25
    fetal movements as predictor of,
      92
    gender differences, 83-89
    habituation, 99
    individuality and, 71-90
    interaction with adults and (*see*
      interaction, babies and
      parents/care-givers)
    marvelous, dynamic, and
      interactive, as descriptives of,
      73-74
Neonatal Behavioral Assessment
    Scale ("the Brazelton"), 73-77,
    84
prediction of, 76-78, 82-83